BUGS
IN
DANGER

**Our Vanishing Bees, Butterflies,
and Beetles**

BUGS
IN
DANGER

Our Vanishing Bees, Butterflies, and Beetles

MARK KURLANSKY

ILLUSTRATED BY JIA LIU

BLOOMSBURY
CHILDREN'S BOOKS
NEW YORK LONDON OXFORD NEW DELHI SYDNEY

BLOOMSBURY CHILDREN'S BOOKS
Bloomsbury Publishing Inc., part of Bloomsbury Publishing Plc
1385 Broadway, New York, NY 10018

BLOOMSBURY, BLOOMSBURY CHILDREN'S BOOKS, and the Diana logo
are trademarks of Bloomsbury Publishing Plc

First published in the United States of America in November 2019
by Bloomsbury Children's Books

Bloomsbury books may be purchased for business or promotional use. For information on bulk purchases
please contact Macmillan Corporate and Premium Sales Department at specialmarkets@macmillan.com

Library of Congress Cataloging-in-Publication Data
Names: Kurlansky, Mark, author. | Liu, Jia (Illustrator), illustrator.
Title: Bugs in danger : our vanishing bees, butterflies, and beetles / by Mark Kurlansky ;
illustrated by Jia Liu.
Description: New York : Bloomsbury, 2019.
Identifiers: LCCN 2019019148 (print) | LCCN 2019022300 (e-book)
ISBN 978-1-5476-0085-4 (hardcover) • ISBN 978-1-5476-0340-4 (e-book)
Subjects: LCSH: Insects—Conservation—Juvenile literature. | Endangered species—Juvenile literature.
Classification: LCC QL467.2.K87 2019 (print) | LCC QL467.2 (e-book) | DDC 595.7—dc23
LC record available at https://lccn.loc.gov/2019019148
LC e-book record available at https://lccn.loc.gov/2019022300

Book design by John Candell
Typeset by Westchester Publishing Services
Printed and bound in the U.S.A. by Berryville Graphics Inc., Berryville, Virginia
2 4 6 8 10 9 7 5 3 1

All papers used by Bloomsbury Publishing Plc are natural, recyclable products made
from wood grown in well-managed forests. The manufacturing processes conform
to the environmental regulations of the country of origin.

To find out more about our authors and books visit www.bloomsbury.com and sign up for our newsletters.

To Charles Darwin and the teachers
who pass on his knowledge

All these sounds, the crowing of cocks,
the baying of dogs, and the hum of insects at noon,
are the evidence of nature's health or *sound* state.
—Henry David Thoreau,
A Week on the Concord and Merrimack Rivers, 1849

CONTENTS

BUGS
IN
DANGER

**Our Vanishing Bees, Butterflies,
and Beetles**

PART ONE

THE iNSECT WORLD

1
FLY SWATTERS

HOW OFTEN DO YOU step on an ant, swat a fly, or slap at a mosquito? On a buggy afternoon, when you're swatting away flies, mosquitoes, and other little beasts, who could blame you for thinking how much better life would be with fewer bugs? To swat an insect is a natural instinct. It is the way we are designed, and it is what is supposed to happen.

Often there are good reasons to get rid of bugs—they bite, they sting, they carry diseases, they destroy crops, and they even eat up houses. But insects are disappearing from the planet at an alarming rate. The intermingling of a huge

number of species is essential for the survival of all animals, including humans. When animals start disappearing, it is a threat to the survival of all of us.

Each life on Earth contributes to other lives on Earth. Sometimes that might just mean another form of life to keep that population in check. So, without ladybugs, there would be too many aphids. These bugs would then devour too many crops, and then we would not have those plants to eat. Life is an enormous interconnected web, and every species adds something. We need them all.

To some, insects are just creepy-crawly things. It is understandable not to like termites, which eat wood and destroy your house, but some people don't even like ants. I had a question for E. O. Wilson, who is an evolutionary biologist and a prominent authority on ants: what should you do when ants enter your home? He said that there was no cause for concern, because they are merely passing through: just allow them some time, and they will usually be gone. (Though, in the meantime, he pointed out that they are particularly fond of tuna fish and whipped cream. But, of course, if you were to make life too nice for them, like some house-guests, they might decide to stay.)

The truth is, though, we are getting fewer bug visitors at home. That's a crisis, because we actually need them there. And we need them in woods and fields and everywhere on Earth.

Insects are part of our landscape. The buzzing in the woods or in a garden tells us nature is alive and well. In tropical rain forests, there are so many insects that it is more than a buzz—almost a roar.

In truth, people tend to like some insects more than others. Tourists gather where fireflies sparkle and where butterflies nest. We will stop our day to watch a bee hovering over a bright and nectar-rich flower or to watch butterflies flickering through a field. We appreciate bees for making us delicious honey. As a child, I spent endless lazy summer hours watching bright two-spotted ladybugs scampering over the birch tree in my family's New England backyard. Butterflies, ladybugs, fireflies, and bees are some of our most beloved insects—and each of these is on the list of vanishing insects. Even if we give little thought to all these small, strange creatures, we are not prepared to live without them.

> *I am set to light the ground,*
> *While the beetle goes his round:*
> *Follow now the beetles hum;*
> *Little wanderer hie thee home.*
> —William Blake

2
HOW BUGS FiT iN

IF WE CARE ABOUT the health of our planet, we can't choose which animals' lives we want to save; we have to care about them all. However, the closer a species is to us humans, the more we seem to care about it.

Nature did not arrange itself into neat separate groups. That was our doing, starting with one man from eighteenth-century Sweden. Carl Linnaeus created a system to organize, name, and classify all living organisms. He identified about 13,000 species, and he expected to eventually classify all of them. He divided living things into categories, ranging from the most general grouping to the most specific: kingdom, phylum, class, order, family, genus, species. You can remember these groups by using the phrase "Kangaroos Play Cellos, Orangutans Fiddle, Gorillas Sing," or "King, Please Come Out, For Goodness Sake," if you prefer.

Linnaeus had no idea how many species there were—and we still don't know. Scientists are constantly discovering new species and new genera. On rare occasions, a whole new kingdom is found. Linnaeus was largely concerned with plants, but animals earned his attention, too. Since his pioneering work, four new kingdoms have been found.

Life is divided into six kingdoms: animals, plants, bacteria, fungi, protists, and archaea. But most of the time we only think about two of these: plants and animals.

Archaea are the simplest organisms and are microscopic. They are made of only a single cell. And that cell has no structure other than the outer cell wall. They were only discovered in 1977, by the American scientist Carl Woese. Once these simple ancient creatures were understood to be an early kingdom, scientists realized that life existed on Earth at least 1 billion years earlier than they had previously thought. Yes, 1 billion years earlier. They might be even older, since they don't require the oxygen-rich air needed by most other forms of life. Archaea make their homes in a wide variety of environments, including lips and colons of the human body. They play an important role in the cycling of carbon and nitrogen, which makes them essential to the cycle of life.

Protists are the next level of organism. They are also made of just one cell, though these cells are more complex. They have a nucleus with genetic material, which means they can pass their characteristics on to offspring but also can evolve changes. The cells are divided into parts called organelles, which have specific functions. Some organelles produce nutrients from sunlight, some generate energy, and some live in oxygen-free environments and do very little. Algae, amoebas, and paramecia are all protists. Amoebas have tentacles for movement, and so do some paramecia. Paramecia, because they are easily grown, are a laboratory favorite. They are oval-shaped and covered with hairlike cilia that allow them to swim through water in any direction at a speed of up to 2 millimeters per second, slightly slower than 24 feet per hour, a respectable speed in their minuscule world, where they travel only millimeters in one direction and so appear to be darting around rapidly. But protists are not adopted as pets or seen very much because they're too small to be seen without a good microscope.

The next kingdom is fungi. Fungi do good and bad things, though we are usually only aware of them when they make trouble—like causing infections such as athlete's foot. But they also break down dead material in nature and recycle the nutrients. Some fungi make useful medicines, such as penicillin (which also provides the blue part of blue cheese!). But mostly we think of the ones we like to eat: the mushrooms.

The next kingdom, bacteria, also includes good and bad members. These organisms are everywhere by the thousands, including in our bodies. Many scientists think bacteria were the first life on Earth; all other life sprang from them. We didn't even know bacteria existed until the seventeenth century, and we did not understand what they did or looked like until the late nineteenth century. That was because a very powerful microscope needed to be invented before humans were able to observe bacteria. Some bacteria cause minor illnesses such as the common cold, chicken pox, and mumps. Others cause deadly diseases such as cholera, pneumonia, and tuberculosis. But there are also bacteria that do helpful things for humans. Generally, helpful bacteria are called probiotics. They are used in medicines but are also available in certain foods. The presence of probiotics is why yogurt is considered healthy. Yogurt contains *Lactobacillus acidophilus*, which is the most commonly used probiotic. But there are many others, such as *Streptococcus thermophilus*, which is found in cheese and helps with digestive ailments.

We tend to focus on the two kingdoms that are easy to see and that include things we like to eat: plants and animals. Plants are multicelled organisms and have unique celluloid walls to those cells, and they usually feed themselves by converting sunlight into energy. Animals are organisms that feed on organic material, have senses and nervous systems, and usually breathe oxygen.

There are about 35 phyla in our animal kingdom. The exact number is not always agreed on. Some consider the tiny brainless worms called

Xenoturbellida a separate phylum, but only two species have been identified, and they seem to have genetic similarities to another phylum. Scientists also debate whether Acoelomorpha, another group of worms, are
a phylum. Some phyla are rejected, some are ignored and forgotten, but
one of the least loved and most widely recognized is Arthropoda, which
includes crayfish, millipedes, centipedes, spiders, and insects. Arthropoda do not have bones. Instead they usually have hard or semihard outer
coverings called exoskeletons. In the nineteenth century, Parisian biologist Étienne Geoffroy Saint-Hilaire, perplexed by this absence of skele-
tons, theorized that the exoskeleton was their vertebrae and that an insect
lived inside its vertebrae. He even speculated that the legs were ribs. He
was wrong about the legs, but the outer casing is what insects have
instead of a skeleton. The insects live within it.

Insects are the class Hexapoda of the phylum Arthropoda. All Hexapoda have very specific characteristics. Insects, distinct from other classes
in the phylum, have six legs. Insects also have bodies divided into three
parts: a head, a thorax, and an abdomen. The heads vary, but all have compound eyes and a pair of antennae used for sensory perceptions such as
smell, touch, wind direction and speed, searching for moisture, and even
taste . . . A compound eye has hundreds or thousands of separate units,
each with its own lens. Each of these units, called an ommatidium, sees in a
slightly different direction. What insects see is a little like a defective televi-
sion screen where the pixels are not completely merged. It results in a some-
what blurred image, but an image that is extremely sensitive to any movement.
This is why it is very difficult to sneak up on an insect (although sometimes
their response to movement is to freeze and hope they are not seen).

Within this group, there is tremendous variety. The *Archimantis mon-
strosa*, a nearly six-inch-long praying mantis that hunts and eats other
insects, is one of them, as is a close but much uglier relative, the
cockroach—as well as the resplendent butterfly, plant-sucking animals

such as aphids, and people-sucking animals like mosquitoes and bed-bugs. The Goliath beetle is not quite as large as an *Archimantis*, but at four inches, it's large enough to have befriended humans and is kept as a pet in parts of Africa, where it can be fed cat or dog food. More than 80 percent of the Earth's animal species are insects.

The most precise category of life is a species. Different types of butterflies or bees or beetles are broken down into different species. A monarch butterfly is a specific species of butterfly, and a honeybee is an identifiable species of bee. These species are identified in biology with two Latin names: one for the genus and the other for the species.

Scientifically, not all insects are bugs. Bugs are a particular order—Hemiptera. They have mouths designed for sucking and are generally either sucking on us (like bedbugs) or sucking crops to death (like aphids). No one likes bugs very much. Even Charles Darwin, the nineteenth-century British scientist who was the founder of modern biology, thought bugs were repulsive. Though he was fascinated by most insects, in his 1845 account of a world voyage on the HMS *Beagle*, he described a large sucking bug in South America as "most disgusting."

Since nobody seems to like bugs, we call any little crawly thing that we don't like a bug. We have become so insistent at overusing this term that scientists have taken to calling Hemiptera "true bugs." But not only aren't all the things we call bugs "true bugs," some aren't even insects. Insects have six legs while spiders, mites, millipedes, and centipedes all have more legs than that. Though they are also from the phylum Arthropoda, these many-legged creatures are not true insects.

But the 1,392,485 species of organisms that are living, named, and described are thought to be only a small part of the actual total. E. O. Wilson estimates that the total number of species is probably between 5 and 30 million. About 20,000 new species are discovered every year. That rate may increase, too, now that there are handheld devices that allow scientists to electronically check DNA against known species.

In the 1980s, samples taken from South American rain forests revealed so many previously unknown insect species that many biologists now estimate that the total number of species may be closer to 30 million. Rain forests, which cover only about 7 percent of the Earth's surface, are thought to contain more than half the world's species, most still undiscovered. But unfortunately, those rain forests are rapidly declining.

Why does this matter? Every single species is valuable because they all possess genes. Genes contain important information about life. A microscopic bacteria has about 1,000 genes. Human beings have about 20,0000–25,000 genes. Surprisingly, some plants have more. Even the microscopic single-celled protists have genes. Genes are often compared to a blueprint. They lay out the design of a species or even of individuals within a species. Variations in genes are how the variations in a species that make evolution possible occur. These variations in genes give a species the ability to adapt to changes in the environment and could be clues to surviving shifts such as climate change.

Life is interdependent, not just among the same phylum but between kingdoms. Every species that is lost threatens other species. It's increasingly understood that insects, plants, and animals greatly depend upon one another for survival. And our survival depends on all of them—including insects.

3

THE DiNNER AND
THE DiNER

MUCH OF OUR UNDERSTANDING of life on the planet, what we call "the natural order," came from Charles Darwin. His most famous book, *On the Origin of Species by Means of Natural Selection, or the Preservation of Favoured Races in the Struggle for Life,* was published in

1859. Since that was too much title for anyone to say or remember, eventually the book became known simply as *On the Origin of Species.* It was Darwin's idea that humans were a species of the animal kingdom, created and operating by the same natural law as other animals. This was one of his most important ideas and a key to understanding modern environmental problems,

ON THE ORIGIN OF SPECIES

including the disappearance of insects. It is important to understand that human beings are not separate from the rest of nature.

Darwin loved insects. When Darwin was a teenager, his cousin William Darwin Fox introduced him to entomology, the study of insects. When he went off to college, Charles wrote his cousin, "I am dying by inches, from not having anybody to talk to about insects." That is a true bugaphile—an insect lover.

Though there have often been arguments and controversy over Darwin's ideas, the more scientists tried to disprove them, the more he's been proven right. One hundred sixty years later, science, including the modern field of genetics, has continued to support most of his theories.

Darwin's most famous idea was evolution. Even Linnaeus did not fully appreciate that the animals he was grouping together by their common traits had those traits because they stemmed from the same roots. Darwin realized that no species came about independently; they all developed out of predecessors. He realized that individual species (not just humans) are obsessed with their own survival, especially reproducing to pass on their genes. To accomplish that, they adapt to any challenges presented, constantly experimenting. The unsuccessful experiments die off, but the successful ones become permanent changes that eventually evolve into new species.

Darwin originally called evolution "descent with modification"—with each generation, changes occur. Millions of crazy ideas get tried out, like a certain kind of butterfly being so colorful that predators can remember it has a bad taste and then avoid eating it. If these strategies are successful, they're kept. We know of a few of these ideas that failed. Dinosaurs were too big and needed too much food, but they had some lasting attributes. Some of them had feathers and hollow bones, making them light. They only needed to be smaller to fly. Today, they are birds.

Among birds, pigeons and doves are examples of very successful species. They can survive and prosper in cities full of people. But on the island of Mauritius, isolated 1,400 miles east of mainland Africa, a variation developed, *Raphus cucullatus*. They grew to be more than 3 feet tall and weigh more than 40 pounds, feeding on local fruit. They had no natural enemies and so had no defenses. They could not even fly. Then people came and brought dogs, cats, pigs, and rats. Now they had many enemies but did not even know to run from them, which is why people called them dodo birds. By the end of the seventeenth century, they were extinct, a variation that could not adapt to change.

Darwin saw nature as a tough and heartless system in which one species advances at the expense of another species. Organisms only care about the survival of their own species, to which end they must live, eat, and reproduce. He wrote, "We do not see, or we forget, that the birds which are idly singing round us mostly live on insects or seeds, and are thus constantly destroying life . . ." Most creatures are both a diner and a dinner. If there are no predators to eat a certain species, that species becomes too populous and, struggling for enough food, becomes highly destructive to another species—or perhaps it might starve. In order to survive, nature always achieves a balance.

Each species only stays in balance if it maintains a large (but not too large) population. A species cannot survive in smaller numbers. Darwin wrote in *On the Origin of Species*, "A large stock of individuals of the same species, relatively to the number of its enemies, is absolutely necessary for its preservation." If for any reason the individuals of a species start dying off, it becomes impossible to predict exactly when there will not be enough individuals for the species to continue. The last few members of the species may die off, or they might possibly be eaten.

But the problem is even worse than that. Every time a species dies off, becomes extinct, it means other species that in some way depend on this species are at risk. And if some of those die off as well, even more species are at risk. Species depend on other species. The system was designed to have millions. Darwin stated it simply: "[T]he greatest amount of life can be supported by great diversification." In other words, the more different kinds of species from all the phyla in all the kingdoms, the more possibilities there are for all kinds of life.

In 1986, at a meeting to discuss this issue, biologists invented the phrase "biodiversity." Biodiversity, a very large number of different species, is essential for the health of the entire system of life sometimes known as the ecosystem. Our current ecosystem is not healthy: we are losing many species, and many other species are declining and may be lost. The disappearance of a few prominent insects could lead to the complete unraveling of life on Earth.

4
THE NATURAL DiSORDER

IT IS DIFFICULT TO say that a species is extinct, especially a small insect that is difficult to find. Scientists are reluctant to pronounce extinction, because one might pop up somewhere. But if there are so few that they cannot be found, extinction is probably not far behind.

The immediate costs of the disappearance of insects are apparent. Many flowering plants depend on insects to spread their pollen, their reproductive material, so that they can produce another generation with their 400,000 genes. Without insects, these plants would disappear, and numerous animals—including humans—would lose this food. Also, some insects prey on other insects—so if one species disappeared, another, lacking natural enemies, might overpopulate and overrun the ecosystem, devastating crops. Insectivores are animals that live by eating insects—these include frogs, some birds, some fish, and some mammals. They would start to die out from lack of food. Then the animals that usually eat the insectivores would start to disappear (we are already seeing a notable decline in birds and frogs). Eventually, even top predators such as wildcats, bears, and humans would lack food.

Why is this crisis happening? In 1962, Rachel Carson published the first widely read environmental book, *Silent Spring*. The book warned that the ecosystem was being destroyed by the indiscriminate use of pesticides, and one pesticide in particular, DDT. Pesticides (which means "killers of pests") are poisons designed to kill particular insects that we do not want, such as mosquitoes that carry the deadly disease malaria. But these poisons might have unintended side effects—they can harm other insects, birds, mammals, and even people.

The crisis Carson was exposing was a relatively simple problem compared with what we are facing today. DDT was being used carelessly and indiscriminately, and this excess was killing insects and birds, with far-reaching consequences for the ecosystem. But now there's not just one answer to what is killing off our insects.

Biologists have labeled the assaults on biodiversity with an acronym—HIPPO.

The first letter, *H*, stands for one of the leading destroyers of insects: habitat loss. This is the single greatest cause of the endangerment and extinction of insect species, as well as other animals and plant species. Since the dawn of civilization, human development has been an assault on nature. Everything we build destroys habitats for wildlife. That is why it is a big mistake for us to imagine the human world and the natural world as separate. There is only one world, one natural order. When we encroach on the territories of the tiger, the panda, the giraffe, or the elk, we soon realize it and try to set aside reserves for these animals. We have even set aside reserves in the ocean to protect sea life.

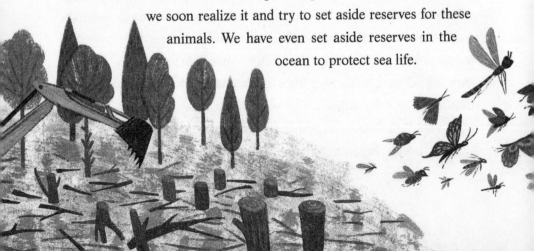

Considerable focus has been placed on the destruction of rain forests. Since this is where we find the single greatest concentration of species on Earth, the clearing of these areas for logging or agriculture (or, in a few cases, such as the Mexico-Guatemala border, the clearing of terrain to secure international borders) is causing by far the greatest destruction of animals and plant species.

But while most of us like the idea of saving the rain forests, we do not want to live in one. Many people prefer not to discuss the places where we do live—how our neighborhoods, shopping malls, suburbs, country homes, highways, and even bike trails are also destroying the natural habitat. The desire of people to live by water—coastlines, lakefronts, and riverbanks—has led to the overdevelopment of these environmentally rich zones. How can California maintain its fruit production when every year thousands of acres of fields are cleared to build housing? Where do we think the insects will live? Most human activity destroys somebody else's habitat, even the most seemingly harmless structures or fields for growing the food we need. Wild habitats are destroyed every year, and this is not just in remote jungles but in the familiar places where we live. Most any use of land—from golf courses to parking lots to airports—destroys wild habitats. Planting fields of crops often threatens the nearby insects that are expected to pollinate these new crops.

The *I* in HIPPO represents invasive species: destructive animals from other places. Hawaii is an example of a place where native plants and birds have been driven close to extinction by outside species that have been brought in either accidentally or intentionally. A native species is kept in check by other native species, but when a foreign species arrives, it may have no enemy. This is a huge problem throughout the world. Among the many examples are foreign bees that destroy native bees, fungi that kill frogs, and mosquitoes that carry diseases that kill birds.

The first *P* is for pollution, and there are many forms destroying many types of life. Pesticides and toxic chemicals that are not well controlled are killing off insects and plants—and have harmful effects on humans, too.

The second *P* is population growth. Here scientists are talking about the human population increasing. This not only leads to more habitat destruction from human activity; it also creates a greater need for human food. When we eat more, we need to farm more. What follows is more destruction of forests, wetlands, and grasslands . . . It is a classic example of how a species that lacks enemies can become outsize and threaten other species.

O is for overharvesting. This is usually associated with overhunting, such as in the case of the destruction of the great American bison herds. It can also mean overfishing. Insects are not immune to this problem. Some insects get harvested for their chemical or medicinal value, or sometimes just their commercial value to collectors, as with butterflies and beetles.

At the first conference on biodiversity, Wilson wrote, "The diversity of life forms, so numerous that we have yet to identify most of them, is the greatest wonder of this planet. The biosphere is an intricate tapestry of interwoven life forms." But we are ripping huge holes in that tapestry, and the disappearance of pivotal insects calls into question the survival of the whole natural system.

HIPPO is missing a letter—*C* for climate change. Most insects are sensitive to weather. Exactly what impact the climate change that we are experiencing is having on insects or the rest of the natural order cannot be said with certainty. In 1859, Darwin, who did not foresee today's weather changes, speculated on the impact of a single country experiencing a change in climate: "The proportional numbers of its inhabitants would almost immediately undergo a change, and some species might become extinct."

5
BEiNG ATTRACTiVE

ONE BIG DIFFERENCE BETWEEN plants and animals is that animals are usually active and plants are usually passive. Just look at reproduction, which all creatures, whether they can think or not, regard as their primary task. Animals generally have elaborate rituals and patterns of activity between males and females to achieve this all-important goal. Plants, by contrast, have strategies. Some plants have seeds that are distributed throughout the countryside, carried by the wind. Other plants circulate their seeds in fruit. Animals eat the fruit and distribute the seeds when they defecate. That is why fruit turns sweet, juicy, and appetizing when its seeds are fully developed, fertile, and ready to be planted somewhere else. The plant needs its seeds to be eaten by animals so they will be distributed. (Of course, fruit-eating birds and mammals do not care about the reproductive process of plants. They just love ripe fruit.)

But where does fruit, which is just the conveyer of seeds, come from? If the plant is what is known as an angiosperm—the scientific name for a plant that flowers—it produces seeds through a complicated process of cooperation between species from different kingdoms. This is known as pollination.

Pollen is the male reproductive material of a flower. Flowers distribute this material as a yellow dust. This makes pollen easy to move. When the pollen of one flower gets to another flower of the same species—if the species is different, this doesn't work—it remoisturizes and swells to its original size. It's still small but more substantial than a fleck of dust. Deposited in the flower's female organs, the pollen then fertilizes and produces seeds.

How pollen dust gets from one flower to another is one of the great wonders of nature. It's also a wonderful example of cooperation between kingdoms: animals carry and distribute the pollen for the plants.

This was yet another revelation by Charles Darwin. The naturalist had observed that plants, just like animals, evolved from lower to higher forms. He reasoned that this would not be possible if they did not cross-breed with other members of their species that were slightly different so that variations would be produced.

He lay on his back in his yard and tried cross-fertilizing flowers—being a human pollinator—by moving the pollen on needles. With thistles and probes and tweezers he prodded and studied the sex lives of flowers. In 1862, three years after his famous *On the Origin of Species*, he published another book with an equally unmusical subtitle: *On the Various Contrivances by Which British and Foreign Orchids Are Fertilised by Insects; and on the Good Effects of Intercrossing*.

He asked why orchids came in so many differs colors, shapes, and sizes, and by examining their sexual organs concluded that they had all evolved to attract different animals to fertilize them. He showed that they were fertilized by a variety of insects such as bees, moths, butterflies, and flies but also by noninsects such as spiders. He observed many different types of apparatus. One orchid had a spot that an insect could push, and as a result two drops of pollen would squirt out and harden. Orchids that attracted moths, which fly in the dark of night, had strong smells. Orchids that attracted butterflies, which fly in daylight, had bright colors. Bees liked yellow and blue flowers, but butterflies were attracted to red and purple.

He also found that pollen stuck to insects as they left flowers, not on entering, and so the pollinator was designed to take the pollen to another plant, not to fertilize the flower that supplied the pollen or even others from the same plant.

Flowers were never looked at the same again. They were devices by which animals could carry out the reproduction of plants.

Plants and animals depend on one another in a variety of ways, but there is no more important example than the fact that flowering plants, which we value not only for their beauty but for their fruit, cannot survive without insects. Often a plant depends on one specific insect.

A wide range of vertebrates and invertebrates perform the all-important task of pollination. These include bats, the only flying mammal, as well as a variety of birds, especially the tiny hummingbird. Numerous insects pollinate, including some butterflies, some moths, some beetles, some flies, and several species of bees.

Flowers have a number of tricks to attract these animals so that they will serve them. They might entice the animals by their good looks: using attractive patterns or colors. Or they might have a delightfully appealing smell. But the flowers' big attraction is nectar.

Nectar is an extremely sweet, concentrated protein that is produced by flowers for the purpose of attracting pollinators. It is not just that these animals love it; they need it. For example, nectar is the entire diet of the honeybee. Female worker bees take it back to their hive, where they make honey from it, which feeds the entire colony. Bats not only eat nectar; they eat pollinating insects found on the flower.

Insects accomplish the overwhelming majority of pollination. It might not be obvious, but Earth is dominated by plants and insects. Insects first appeared more than 400 million years ago, and until recently scientists had thought that plants began around the same time.

It is now believed plants first appeared about 700 million years ago, even then newcomers to a world of fungi, mushrooms, and yeast, which started up some 1,300 million years ago. Plants and insects grew up together, working with one another in a world long before dinosaurs existed, a world with neither birds nor mammals. This world also had no flowers: they evolved recently, only 130 million years ago.

Darwin played an important role in our understanding of the connection between kingdoms. They are not separated, and neither is their evolution. Darwin believed that if it could be traced, it would be found that all organisms had a common ancestry. They could all, regardless of which kingdom they came from, be traced back to a founding organism, probably a bacteria. Since the discovery of DNA, the connection between plants and animals has been established because they have about 70 percent of the same DNA. In other words, only 30 percent of what makes an animal is different from what makes a plant.

Scientists debate which came first: flowers or pollinators. The oldest fossils of bees are 80 million years old, and the oldest fossils of flowers are 120 million years old. But fossils are not conclusive evidence. There may be older fossils that have never been found or organisms that never fossilized. Now scientists are considering the possibility that bees were around 140 million years earlier than originally thought. After all, many other insects were already around then. The oldest known flowers were all pollinated by bees, flies, beetles, biting moths, and thrips. Thrips are tiny insects considered pests by gardeners because they feed on plants.

According to fossils found in the Basque mountains of northern Spain, thrips may have been the first pollinators.

But millions of years before flowers and pollination, insects and plants were working together to assure their survival. Ants, one of the world's most numerous insects, have long worked with plants, spreading their seeds and enriching the soil. Ants, like beetles, are carnivorous insects. They eat other animals, feeding on herbivorous insects (insects that feed on plants). Ants keep those populations in check so that they don't completely kill off plant populations. Even termites and wood-boring beetles, destroyers of wood, are helpful to plants. They turn dead plant matter into valuable nutrients in the soil that are then absorbed through the roots of plants.

The stamen is a flower's male part. It holds grains of pollen, which have to get to an ovule to fertilize it. Within a flower's pistil—its female part—the ovary contains ovules, a flower's equivalent of eggs. If the ovules are fertilized, they develop into seeds.

Plants and insects have coevolved. This means that both have adopted changes designed to work in their specific relationship. All flowers have mostly the same parts, but they are arranged differently depending on who their pollinators are. Some flowers are indiscriminate, just standing there, open to any pollinator who comes by. But other plants have flowers adapted to specific pollinators. They have designed their nectar stores, their pollen, and their male and female organs in a way that only one species of insect knows how to get at them.

Pollinating animals exhibit specific preferences for format, size, shape, color, and smell, while flowers evolved to appeal to the preferences of their choice pollinators. Though the giant Amazonian water lily carries a rich supply of nectar, just one species of scarab beetle is attracted to it. Bees choose flowers by scent and color. They like the same aromas that we do, but they are red color-blind, so most bees are not interested in red flowers. They are drawn to yellow, blue, blue green, and violet. Butterflies, on the other hand, see more colors than we do and are drawn to a wide range of colors.

The nineteenth-century German poet Heinrich Heine wrote: "With the rose the butterfly's deep in love."

The garden pea blossom is either pink or white. It has a large, bright, fanlike petal sticking up vertically. This is called the banner petal, there to flag down any searching honeybee. The garden pea has a pattern of stripes that point the way down to their reproductive organs in the same way the lines on a runway help guide planes to land. The flower has two wing petals that fold together at the top to make a protective covering in the shape of a pup tent. The honeybee lands on a small petal in front of them, the keel petal, designed to be a honeybee landing strip. Once landed, the bee spreads open the wing petals to get at the organs. No other insect knows how to do that, and so the snow peas save themselves exclusively, modestly draped, for the honeybees.

If the honeybees stop coming, that is the end of the peas. No one else can help them. They have no way to reproduce. Another species of pollinator would not even attempt it. These pollinator-specific plants are the most vulnerable to extinction. They show the most signs of dwindling in numbers.

Flowers evolve to suit certain pollinators, and this is why there is such a tremendous variety of blossoms. There are 250,000 known species of flowering plants today, a tremendous diversity. Sixty-five million years ago there were only about 22,000 species. In the past 50 million years, flowers have become more complicated, with rings and tubes and other advanced structures. That is because vertebrates started getting into pollination—hummingbirds, orioles, bats, possums, opossums, lizards, lemurs, and even monkeys. Even human beings pollinate, though they have been the least effective. From a palace in what is today northern Iraq, there is a stone carving from between 883 and 859 BCE showing date blossoms being manually pollinated by rubbing pollen onto female flowers. Date palms are dioecious, which means each palm is either male or female. Even today, in parts of Iraq, Iran, Syria, and Egypt, it's an annual tradition in the springtime to remove pollen from male date palms and place it in the flowers of female palms.

Different animals approach pollination differently. While most pollinators are female, not all of them are. Industrious male mosquitoes are off in the swamp pollinating flowers while the females buzz around us, sucking our blood and being annoying. Often in the insect world, the females get the more dangerous job. Beetles are much messier about it than bees. Some beetle species have what seems like pollination parties, in which a number of beetles pile into the same flower, taking bites out of leaves and petals and defecating on the flowers.

Flies are also important pollinators, though we don't seem to like them much more than we like mosquitoes. Their order, Diptera, contains 45 families of pollinating species. In fact, the four largest orders of insects are all pollinators—Diptera; Hymenoptera, which includes wasps and bees; Coleoptera, which are beetles; and Lepidoptera, which includes moths and butterflies.

In today's world, most pollinating insects are experiencing a decrease in their numbers and a narrowing of the geographic area in which they can live. Most pollinating plants that have been studied are producing fewer seeds. When fewer pollinators visit plants, they produce fewer seeds.

In areas with a decline in pollinating insects, the number of plants decreases. They do not have enough flowers to attract pollinators. From above, the flying scout bee searches for stands with huge numbers of flowers. If the crop is no longer large enough, the scout skips over it. Eventually these plants will die off because they cannot reproduce. And then how many animals that depend on these plants' fruits or seeds for food (including us) will go hungry? And what of the animals that depend on those animals?

If pollinators, mostly insects, were to die off, flowering plants would not survive. They could not reproduce. Of course, this would mean a world with no flowers and no honey, but it would be even worse than that. We humans depend on grains and fruits for food. Eighty percent of the plants that provide us with food depend on pollination. The livestock we raise for food also depends on pollinating plants for food. Without them, it would be very difficult to raise meat and dairy products. It is estimated that about a third of all the food we eat depends on pollination. And it is not only food. Cotton also depends on honeybees.

This disappearance of insects is not only a disaster for plants but a calamity for human life.

PART TWO
BEES

6
A CHARMER WiTH A STiNG

MANY PEOPLE FEAR BEING stung by bees. Bee stings can be painful for a number of minutes, and for people who are allergic, stings can be dangerous or even—though rarely—deadly. But most bees pose little threat to people. Usually a bee that stings is a female worker involved in the nectar-pollen business. Male bees have no stingers. A hive's queen bee, while she does have a stinger, almost never leaves the hive except to reproduce, and on these occasions, she has a single purpose and is not thinking about you.

Forager bees out scouting or pollinating also have more important things on their minds and are unlikely to sting you. But a guard bee or even a forager might decide to sting you if you are near the hive, because they have an instinct to protect it. These bees have a barbed stinger, an extra little point like the barb on a fishing hook that keeps the hook in the fish's mouth.

When they sting other insects, a bee's stinger slides in and out, but when a bee attacks a mammal, the barb catches on its thick skin. When they try to fly away, the stinger stays behind—and often, so does much of the abdomen—and the bee dies. Even if it survives, it will never again have a stinger. It is not certain if the bee weighs this usually fatal decision to sting you, or if she is just not aware of the severe consequences of stinging a mammal.

The abandoned stinger now stuck in you continues pumping a painful poison, apitoxin. It would seem that the best solution would be to remove the stinger as quickly as possible. But if you rub it, swat it, or pull on it, that pushes out more poison and causes more pain. There is a way to get a fingernail between the venom sac and the stinger and drag it over the skin, but if you don't know how to do this, the best thing is to leave it alone. With such a small supply of venom, the pain won't last longer than about 10 minutes.

We forgive them. We like bees. They are cute in their chubby black-and-yellow striped outfits, and by pollinating and by providing us with honey, they render us a huge service. Also, we admire their organization. Some see a hive as a honey-nectar company: hardworking, well organized, and productive. But then some others see it as more of a cooperative, where everyone works for the common good. Regardless of how one categorizes bee society, bees are industrious, dedicated, and beneficial.

The oldest known bee lived 100 million years ago and died in a pool of tree sap that fossilized into amber in what is now Myanmar. It was much smaller than the bees of today and covered with fur for pollen collecting. The big disappointment is that this ancient insect appears to have been a loner without the social order of bees that captures our attention and admiration. Traces of earlier bees are always found single and alone. These days there is still a small percentage of bees—about 4,000 species—that do not live in organized societies.

When humans first started raising bees for honey thousands of years ago, they viewed a beehive as a monarchy, because these early beekeepers expected well-run societies to be monarchies run by royalty. Since men expected successful societies to be run by males, they mistakenly called the hive's queen bee a king. Even Aristotle, the brilliant Greek philosopher from the fourth-century BCE, called the head bee a king bee. It was only later discovered that the king bee was a female, and then it became a queen bee. But the queen bee does not resemble a ruling monarch.

Twenty-five thousand bee species have been cataloged, and another 40,000 have been discovered but not yet named. The order to which bees belong is Hymenoptera, which also includes wasps and ants. There are more than 110,000 Hymenoptera species in the world that have been identified and named. Biologists believe this is a small fraction of the number that exist, which is estimated to be about 3 million—but this is only a guess. As you are reading this, one or two unknown species may be becoming extinct.

A queen bee's job is not to be a wise ruler but to constantly reproduce. The male bee, the drone, meets the queen outside of the hive to mate and then dies immediately after. (The drone cannot assure his survival just by avoiding this fatal act; once winter sets in, any drones that are still alive are thrown out of the hive and left to starve.)

The queen flies back to the hive, which is divided into small wax holes called cells. The cells are used to store honey, but in the fall, the queen uses empty cells toward the middle of the hive, where it is warmest, to deposit fertilized eggs, one egg per cell. The workers flap their wings and burn energy to create heat so that a temperature of almost 97 degrees Fahrenheit is maintained in the center of the hive, a warm and cozy room on a winter's day.

Fertilized eggs will become female bees. Drones are produced from unfertilized eggs. Drones need wider cells, and the workers who make the cells place wider ones around the outside of the hive. There can be no more drones than there are wide cells.

Also, workers accept or reject eggs by eating the ones they don't want hatched. So it is the female workers, not the queen bee, who really decide the community's female-male ratio. Once the queen places the eggs, her work is done until she produces more.

One of the differences between our phylum, Chordata, and the insect phylum, Arthropoda, is that we give birth to miniature versions of ourselves, whereas Arthropoda begin as completely different creatures— larvae, cocoons, and other strange things that eventually change into adults. It is called metamorphosing. This is why Chordata have cute babies and insects don't.

Bee eggs become a caterpillar-like creature known as a "larva." Three days later, the worker bees secrete a substance called royal jelly and feed it to the larvae. After yet another three days, they start feeding the larvae pollen and honey. When a larva is around 10 days old, it completely fills the cell and spins an outer casing. The workers then cover this cell— containing a pupa, or cocoon—with wax. About a week later, the animal, now a fully formed bee, eats its way out of the waxed-up cell.

The queen is the mother of most of the hive's bees. She works hard, not ruling the hive, but getting fertilized and laying eggs. She can lay

2,000 eggs per day. Some of the females are scouts seeking out the best flowers; some are foragers, gathering the nectar; some guard the hive; and other bees keep the hive clean to prevent viruses and diseases. Some of the females might also try to become queens. But there is only room in each hive for one queen, so the hopefuls fight one another until a winner orders the bees to move to a new hive. The original queen can also order a new hive. Everything else the other bees do without her orders, while she is busy producing more bees.

Bees bring many skills to their work. They have a very strong sense of smell through their antennae. Bees also have extremely fast vision. Bumblebees have the fastest color vision of any animal in the kingdom. It is thought to be five times faster than human vision. An image of light grabbed by their eyes goes to the brain with remarkable speed. Scientists measure what is called the flicker-fusion rate—that's the speed at which flickers of light can be perceived as individual flashes before they reach a speed where they instead look like one continuous light. Humans can perceive 16 flickers per second, but a bee can distinguish 300 per second. This does not mean a lot if you are looking at a tree. But if you are a bee looking at moving objects or when you are a moving object, this is a tremendously valuable trait.

In baseball, batters have an advantage if they can recognize the type of pitch before it gets to the plate. Ballplayers with bumblebee eyes would be unstoppable. They would gaze at the ball and perceive each revolution of the spin. A 95-mile-per-hour fastball would look like it was flying through the air in slow motion. And if there was any movement on the pitch, if it curved left or right or sunk or rose, a bee-eyed batter would detect that movement as the ball appeared in different tiny lenses of the mosaic of compound vision.

Bees are extremely sensitive to motion because their compound vision offers 4,500 separate lenses in each eye of the worker bee. The queen has about 1,000 fewer lenses. With the goal of finding a queen in flight before another drone gets to her, a drone has about 3,000 more images than the queen. But these images are not detailed. Insects see the world as a mosaic in which each tile has an unclear image but strong color, and for them the total picture is rapidly changing.

Swift vision allows bees to be extremely perceptive, not only quickly memorizing landmarks for a return flight but in spotting just the right flowers as they buzz by. They see not just the flowers but their structure, too. With their ultraviolet vision, they perceive colors and spots and lines on certain petals that give them landing guidance or that direct their way toward nectar. While zooming past, bees see a flower in greater detail and more color than we do just standing and staring at one.

7
HONEY, I'M HOME

IN NATURE, A SPECIES tends to care only for its own. Insects do not plan or intend to gather pollen and distribute it to other flowers. When one species helps another, it is usually in the course of trying to do something for itself. If insects were tidier animals, they might be able to fly into a flower, get its nectar, and fly out without even touching the pollen. But the flower makes such an operation very difficult, so the pollinator has to dig in and get messy.

This is why the bee is a particularly good pollinator. When out on a mission to gather nectar, the roundish furry body can't help

but get pollen dust stuck to it. They get it all over themselves. A bee may try to shake or kick off the messy pollen, but inevitably some sticks in hard-to-reach places—like the middle of the back, the top of the head, or even between the eyes. When the bees travel to the next flower and dig past its petals—crawling, shimmying sideways for the sweet nectar—they accidentally rub pollen dust onto the new flower's female organs. That's how the ovules get fertilized to make a seed.

A poodle and a cocker spaniel can be bred to produce a mix that some call a cockapoo. That is because they are different breeds but the same species. But you cannot cross a poodle with a cat and get a kittypoo, because species of different genera cannot fertilize one another. Therefore, if the bee brings pollen from one species of flower to a different species of another genus, no fertilization takes place.

This does not concern the bee in the least. She is not trying to reproduce flowering plants. She is only trying to gather nectar, but, fortunately for the plants, she is very particular about which nectar she gathers.

The western honeybee, *Apis mellifera*, is also known as the Euopean honeybee. It is the most famous bee, celebrated as an extremely industrious nectar gatherer and, in turn, an extremely productive honey maker. In the course of a year, a single hive of honeybees may gather nectar from 500 million carefully chosen flowers.

Humans have been robbing beehives of their honey for a very long time. Not only the honey is valuable; humans have also found uses for the wax bees make to build their hives. For centuries, beeswax was the only wax we used. We crafted candles from it, and it was used for writing on and for sealing packages. Even mummies in ancient Egypt were sealed tight with beeswax. Today, with less expensive substitutes available, there are still countless commercial uses for beeswax.

Rock paintings in Zimbabwe and South Africa from when humans were only hunter-gatherers and had not learned to cultivate food show

There are 11 known species of *Apis* bees, all of which are native to either Europe or Asia, and all of them are quite different. The *Apis dorsata*, the native Asian honeybee, is a giant: almost an inch long. The *Apis mellifera*, the standard European honeybee, is also known as the western honeybee. Though by no means one of the smaller bees, it is half the size of its huge Asian cousin. None of the honeybees are native to the Americas.

the gathering of honey by smoking bees out of their hives, a technique still used today.

Cruder methods are also recorded in northern Spain, seen in rock paintings that are 10,000 years old. It seems the honey gatherer would climb a tree with a basket and just stick a hand into the hive. Given the honeybee's instinct to protect its hive, this was almost certainly an unpleasant and painful task for the honey gatherer.

The African smoking technique would have worked better. The trick of the smoke is that it sedates the bees, making them very calm. No one knows why. Some have speculated that it is a learned response to avoid panic in forest fires. Others speculate that it is because fires deprive the air of oxygen, which makes bees have less energy.

For many centuries in Europe, honey and ripe fruit were the only sources of sweetness. When Persians invaded India in 510 BCE, they discovered sugar and called it "the reed that gives honey without bees." But most Europeans did not have sugar until the thirteenth or fourteenth century, and so honey, and the little *Apis mellifera,* were vital to their diets.

They even made a beer-like alcoholic beverage, mead, from fermented honey. In a tradition going back to the ancient Egyptians, the Greeks, and then the Romans, a newlywed couple drank mead for a month to bring good fortune to their marriage. This is the origin of the word honey-moon, a month of honey.

Bees do not make wax and honey for us. Wax is the building material for their homes, and honey is their protein-rich food. But humans want the result of their labors, so *Apis mellifera* have been transplanted all over the world, including throughout North America, where billions of bees have adapted to the many climates of the continent. During the more than three centuries honeybees have been in North America, they have prospered over other competitors, including native bees and wasps, because they are such extraordinarily efficient nectar gatherers, which gives them strength but also makes them great pollen distributors.

They were an invasive species that was never regretted. They were brought over, they were highly successful, and both people and the natural order seemed to prefer them to the locals they displaced.

8

BEE MOVIE

THERE ARE WINNERS AND losers in the natural order. The losers become extinct and their genes vanish. All living organisms are programed to fight as hard as they can to not let that happen.

Apis mellifera was introduced to North America in 1622, by Europeans who wanted to continue the honey industry they knew in Europe. Honeybees were completely unknown in the Americas, and the native people called them "the white man's fly." At the time, there were about 5,000 native pollinating species in North America, but the population had expanded in the wild, which is called a feral population. But from 1859 until 1922, seven subspecies were introduced. Four of these failed, and disease also decimated the feral population, so today descendants of the three successful strains (not related to the original 1622 bees) have become the dominant American pollinator.

It is hard to stay on top. In 1956, honeybees from South Africa were brought to Brazil. These were heartier bees than the local western honeybees, and the hybrid that resulted from intermingling the two proved even more resistant to disease and mites. Because the new bees were from

South Africa, the hybrid was called the Africanized bee, or Neotropical African bee. However, they are increasingly known as killer bees because these crossbreeds are extremely aggressive. Not only are they much more likely to sting, but in a few cases, they have ganged up on a beekeeper or an animal and stung them to death. It's not that these bees are larger or have stronger venom. Quite the opposite: these African bees are smaller, so they produce less venom. However, they are more prone to stinging and have a strong territorial urge to protect the hive, which they sometimes do by swarming and attacking all at once. A person can survive about ten stings for every pound of body weight, so deaths do not happen often. Still, these aggressive insects have killed several hundred people.

The image of swarms of killer bees traveling up the continent killing everyone in their path has been greatly exaggerated in science-fiction stories and horror movies. There have been numerous low-budget films (amusingly, they are known as B movies) about killer bees, including *The Savage Bees* (1976), *Terror Out of the Sky* (1978), and *The Swarm* (1978). As this new hybrid traveled north, honey production declined because many beekeepers refused to work with these pushy bees. But when new beekeepers learned to work with Africanized bees, honey production came back. Gradually, the Africanized bees have been replacing milder European bees in the Americas.

All these competing species are social animals struggling for their own groups. The individual that is conflicted between his own good and the good of the group is from a later stage in evolution that biologists think has happened much less frequently. One such species is humans. As humans go forward, unless something has gone terribly wrong in their evolution, they must, as social animals, have an urge to protect so that their group can survive. But they also have a strong urge to promote themselves as individuals and work toward their own prosperity. Should I make a fortune and live well selling oil even if the oil threatens the future of humankind? Bees have no such internal conflicts or dilemmas about what to do. Each bee cares only for the good of its own group. Bees do not concern themselves with their individual lives or futures, only with the survival and prosperity of their group.

9
WHY BEES BOOGiE

BEES HAVE A REGIMENTED society, and every bee in a hive community has an assigned task: the scouts, the nectar collectors, the forager bees, the guards of the hive, and the cleanup crew. All of them are female, and they are completely dedicated to their jobs. The rear legs of foragers are built with rakes, brushes, and baskets for pollen, because bees, unlike all other insects, are not content with merely gathering nectar to eat. They also gather pollen to take back to the hive to consume. They store extra pollen (which is not used in pollination) on their legs. Some bees also gather pollen using aprons made of their own hair; these are on their bellies and act like Velcro. All in all, bees acquire a lot of pollen. Some they give to other flowers, but that is not their goal. They're looking for food for their group.

Observers often see a large swarm of forager bees heading straight for a choice set of blossoms. How do the bees know where to go? For centuries, this was a great mystery. Bees often fly for miles and then proceed straight to a flower they seem to have known would be right there. They do not wander around, searching for just the right flower, but fly directly to the desired one. Actually, someone told them, but it took centuries for humans to discover who or how.

For most bees, nectar gathering is a community project. They plan and plot their nectar campaigns and, in a bee kind of way, talk about it. Of course, bees do not exactly talk, but as highly social animals, they have a number of ways to communicate with other members of their community. They convey some knowledge with a variety of buzz patterns by using their antennae. They may also emit a variety of smells to communicate information to other hive members. Bees also use dance. Among one genus, *Apis*, dancing is the leading means of communication.

Aristotle closely studied bees and concluded that there must be a leader guiding them to just the right spot to gather nectar. For centuries, this was the accepted fact, but Aristotle was wrong. The truth would not be known until Austrian scientist Karl von Frisch began studying bees in 1919.

Today the study of bees is quite popular, in part because of von Frisch, but in the early twentieth century, few scientists were studying them. The Austrian scientist noticed something odd about honeybees: not all the foragers have the same task. Some are scouts who go out first and survey the territory. Von Frisch noticed that when a scout returned to the nest, all the other foragers stood around her in a packed circle at the hive's entrance, a kind of foyer. It was as though the scouting bee was giving a speech. Actually, she is, but instead of with words or sounds, she communicates with movement. She dances her story, telling the others exactly where she found the big caches of nectar. Von Frisch observed that a bee that is only a half inch in size can fly more than six miles to a specific flower and find her way back home, observing compass direction, altitude, the topography of the passing landscape—all the information needed to find the flower again.

He identified a full repertoire of dances—the round dance, the tail-wagging dance, the jostling dance, the spasmodic dance, the sickle dance, the grooming dance, the jerking dance, and the trembling dance. Von Frisch named the dances for what they looked like, but each dance was designed to communicate on a different subject.

The round dance begins with the dancing scout taking rapid running-like steps in a tiny circle only the size of a single cell of the hive. She repeats this circle several times before completely reversing her direction. The dance might last for only 2 reversals but more typically there are about 20.

Round Dance

Then there is a break, an intermission in the performance.

Von Frisch never called it an intermission, but the dancer stops, some honey is served, all the foragers eat, and after, the dance resumes. As the scout bee spins, she caters to her audience, making sure that everyone is paying attention. She brushes by them, and they tuck their antennae underneath and start circling behind her, imitating her steps. It's like a dance class. When the scout's dance steps and reversals are over, the foragers take flight and travel to the luscious flowers they have been told about.

Von Frisch estimated that the round dance could give only enough information for flowers up to 100 meters (or 328) feet away. But if there are flowers worth the effort, honeybees will travel much farther.

To communicate long-distance missions, the scout performs her tail-wagging dance. In this dance, the performing scout runs fiercely in a straight line and then stops and returns in a semicircle, follows the straight course again, and then makes a semicircle back around the other

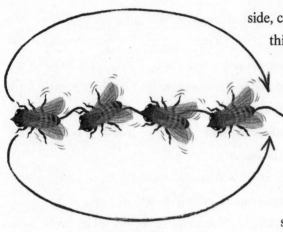

Tail-Wagging Dance

side, creating a circle. She does this over and over. She starts shaking the tip of her abdomen but not moving her head. What von Frisch called tail wagging could also be called butt shaking. He timed 13 to 15 shakes a second. Von Frisch noted that this was accompanied by buzzing.

The performance creates a great deal of excitement. Shy bees stand around the far outside of the circle, but some of the inner circle form a kind of conga line, following the scout in a circle, shaking their behinds in rhythm.

A jostling run is a celebration after a successful mission. The scout bee runs through the crowd of fellow foragers, bumping them as she goes. A shaking dance, also called a grooming dance, occurs when the other foragers help clean the scout covered in pollen or dirt.

Jostling Run

These dances are a kind of language in which important information is communicated. From hive to hive, the dances vary. These slight differences are said to be "dialects" of the dance languages.

Bees travel enormous distances with the information they have learned about flowers: their sizes, shapes, colors, and exact location. It is not clear how they measure distance. It is not by flying time, because if a strong wind slows them down or speeds them up, they compensate for it and still manage to arrive at their target. We know they sometimes recognize landmarks along the way, such as a large tree or a building that they learned about from the dance.

Not surprisingly, von Frisch's fantastic findings were greeted with both amazement and skepticism. That is how science works. Scientists are trained to doubt, and the great ideas of science are all met with other scientists who say the new idea is wrong. They might say the methodology is flawed and the conclusions are false. This also happened with Darwin's theory of evolution, Pasteur's germ theory, and Einstein's theory of relativity. But scientific doubters often end up strengthening an idea. When trying to prove it wrong, with tougher examinations, they sometimes find out not only that the original research was right, but they may enhance the understanding of it. This is exactly what happened with Von Frisch's dancing bees.

In the 1960s, two California scientists, Adrian Wenner and Patrick Wells, challenged von Frisch's findings and started conducting new experiments to disprove him. But they ended up only confirming most of his findings and then learned even more. In 1973, Karl von Frisch was awarded the Nobel Prize for his studies of bee dances.

Others have continued his work, such as his student Martin Lindauer. But there is still much we don't know about bee behavior. Why are some missions for nectar unsuccessful? Was the information sometimes off a bit, or did the bees just not pay attention? Why didn't other types of bees or other social insects such as wasps develop these dancing skills? Are all dancers the same or, as with human dancers, are some more talented than others? Are dancing scouts born or chosen for their talent among foragers?

Bees are the great intellectuals of the insect world. Numerous other scientists have demonstrated the extreme sophistication, intelligence, and ability of these remarkable little animals. In one experiment, bees were exposed to certain scents at certain times of day, and the following day at those exact times, most knew what smells to seek.

But despite all this, life for them is a constant struggle.

10
THE STRUGGLE
OF BEEiNG

A HONEYBEE HIVE IS a delicate thing. If we wish to use it, we must proceed with utmost care.

The primitive human technique of climbing a tree and robbing a wild hive of its honey is extremely destructive to bee society. An invaded hive becomes unlivable, and its queen needs to lead her bees to a new location. This move is not an easy one and is a huge waste of resources; along the way, the hive abandons unhatched larva, wax, and nectar. Also, a new hive must be built before the onset of winter. If a hive is robbed of its honey late in the season, there may not be enough time to rebuild, and the bee colony will die.

Transporting hives to agricultural areas was a technique invented by the Egyptians by 2400 BCE. For centuries that followed, hives used to pollinate farm fields were cultivated in baskets. After the bees did their work and the crops were harvested, the beehives were destroyed to gather their honey. This changed in 1851, when an American clergyman named Lorenzo Lorraine Langstroth patented the modern artificial beehive. He constructed it from a wooden champagne case. A number of vertical

frames slid into the crate, and the bees constructed wax hives on them. Since Langstroth's invention, maintaining man-made hives has become a flourishing industry around the world.

Every year, trucks carrying about 500 hives are moved from field to field for polli- nation. On the East Coast, they are brought to Florida for the citrus crop, then north for apples and cherry blos- soms, and then all the way up to Maine for blueberries.

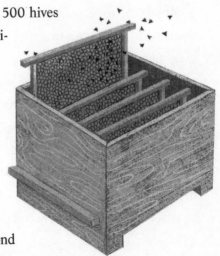

With around one million acres of almond trees, California has become the largest almond producer in the world. To pollinate their trees, almond growers need at least 30 billion honeybees—brought in every February from as far away as Australia.

Farmers grow alfalfa because the grain's high protein content helps their cows produce more milk. In the early twentieth century, American farmers in Utah, Idaho, and neighboring states discovered that the little alkali bee, the *Nomia melanderi*, also favored alfalfa. In these desert areas, newly irrigated fields were promising habitats for pollinators.

The alfalfa blossom is a tricky one: first, its keel petal needs to be released to spread the wing petals and expose the well-protected reproductive organs. Alkali bees are experts at this, and these desert dwellers earned their name through choosing salty, dry areas, nesting on the ground.

In the 1950s, farmers learned to move soil with nesting alkali bees in trays into the alfalfa-growing areas. Farmers discovered they could up their alfalfa harvest by bringing in more alkali bees, which is how Idaho became the third most milk-producing state in the United States.

More alkali bees were brought in. The bees, the alfalfa, and the dairy all became huge industries. By 1990, alfalfa had become a $5-billion-a-year business. Alfalfa seeds were sold around the world. Everyone wanted to grow alfalfa, so farmers plowed up more and more land to grow it. In doing that, they forgot to leave habitat for the ground-nesting bees—and then there were fewer bees and less alfalfa. A downward cycle began. As alkali bees became scarce, farmers hoped that bumblebees, another North American native, could to be brought in to do the work. But it turns out that bumblebees, though they pollinate alfalfa, are not very good at it.

Then the alfalfa was attacked by the lygus bug, a vegetarian insect that lives by sucking the sap from plants. Farmers started spraying pesticides to get rid of the lygus. It is not certain, but the pesticide may have also contributed to reducing the bee population.

Honeybees may have great eyes for batting in baseball, but as players they would probably spend too much time on the injured list. They are smart but fragile animals. They have weak resistance to both diseases and poisons.

A farmer who works with crops and insects must perform a constant balancing act with nature. Biologists talk of "the law of unintended consequences"—once you start tinkering with the natural order, it is difficult to predict what changes this will cause. When alfalfa farmers brought in a sturdier bee, the Canadian leafcutter, these colonies were attacked by chalkbrood, a fungus that attacks the bees in their helpless larva stage.

There were other problems. In the late twentieth century, numerous diseases and parasites arrived. Many bees, including the European honeybee, have been falling prey to various vermin and mites. One major problem is the *Varroa* mite. This mite attaches itself to a bee and sucks out the animal's hemolymph, the circulating liquid in insects that is their equivalent of blood. For this reason, they are sometimes called bee vampires. This tiny creature is too small to see except as a dot—but if you could get a closer look, you would see a faceless creature that resembles a hairy fingernail and seems like an extraterrestrial.

The aptly named *Varroa destructor* mite probably lived in harmony with bees for millions of years. But when the honeybee first came into contact with the *Varroa* mite, probably in Russia in the 1950s, it spread to Asia and Eastern Europe and eventually the Americas. It arrived in the United States in 1987.

The problem with an invasive species is that it spreads uncontrolled because its natural enemies do not come along with it. Of course, the honeybee is also an invasive species not native to the Americas—so one invader that we like was being attacked by one that we didn't.

Honeybees in North America have been plagued by the tracheal mite that attacks the respiratory system, and in some areas, these mites have killed as much as half the population. There is also a parasite that lodges in the honeybee's stomach, weakening them and causing many to die.

From South America, the small hive beetle has launched an invasion. In its larva stage, the wormlike creature has not yet blossomed into a full-grown beetle and eats honey, pollen, and young bees. Unless a bee-keeper discovers them in time, these hive beetles destroy beehives. Bees have their own security force that can drive out some enemies, such as the half-inch wax moth, but if the bees fail to eject them from the hive they can destroy the colony.

Pesticides sprayed by farmers to kill insects that are destroying their crops may also accidentally kill bees. This happened in Washington state in 1973, when a badly managed pesticide spraying killed alkali bees in their nesting grounds. The result was a huge decline in the production of alfalfa seeds. When a plant is sprayed with an insecticide, the poison might keep away insects that harm the plant, but the plant may also store this poison in its flower. A bee might harvest this poisonous nectar and carry it back to its hive, proving deadly to an entire colony.

This is the law of unintended consequences. If you try to alter nature, if, for example, you decide to kill a species because it seems to be a pest, it is difficult to predict what all the consequences of this action will be.

11
THE VANiSHING ACT

SINCE 2004, HONEYBEES HAVE been disappearing from hives. If this were happening in one place, say the almond groves of California or Maine's blueberry bogs, scientists might be able to identify what was causing the disappearances and correct it. But this has been happening all over the United States, Canada, Europe, Asia, and South America.

As we have seen, bees and other insects are endangered for various reasons. It's certainly not just honeybees. Native bees in North America, which are still essential for the pollination of 130,000 species of flowering plants, have also been losing large portions of their population to mites and pesticides.

But since 2004 there has been a different kind of disappearance. The forager honeybees may leave the hive and never come back, leaving the queen and drones to starve. With pesticide poisoning, the bees are normally found dead—but these days, bees are simply disappearing. They just fly off and do not return. Some hives are completely abandoned, even though their storage section is full of honey and nectar. Sometimes unhatched eggs are found in the abandoned hive. We don't know why bees would leave behind their hard-fought treasure of food—or their young, who were the future of the species.

The phenomenon is named colony collapse disorder, more commonly called CCD. Many scientists originally believed it was an epidemic, an outbreak of a virus. But which viruses, and what caused the outbreak? Perhaps, some theorized, it was a new strain of virus that attacked the bees' immune systems, leaving them vulnerable to diseases.

CCD has led to some dire predictions. It is estimated that at the current rate, the United States might be without honeybees by the year 2035. If that happens, it would cause a massive decline in US agriculture and the American food supply. But that is just one of many predictions; since there is no agreement on what is causing the disappearances, these ominous forecasts are not reliable.

This is not the first unexplained die-off of bees. However, the die-offs seem to be getting bigger. In 1896, one happened just in Colorado. In 1917, it was Ontario, Ohio, New York, and New Jersey. In the 1970s, what was called the "disappearing disease" occurred in 27 states.

As investigations of this new outbreak have spread around the world, more and more theories have been offered to explain this distressing turn of events. Could there be an outbreak of parasites, some of which have always plagued bees? One popular theory held that cell phone transmissions were jamming the navigational system of bees, and some postulated that terrorist groups were killing off bees to destroy agriculture.

Cell phones were quickly eliminated when it was realized that CCD attacked in areas that lacked cell phone reception. The terrorist theory had absolutely no evidence. Scientists in affected areas developed plausible theories, but unfortunately other scientists found equally plausible reasons to reject these theories too.

A leading suspect was pesticides. These chemicals were originally developed during World War II as an outgrowth of experiments with chemical weapons. Once chemists learned they could engineer these chemicals to target insects, they developed a pesticide against mosquitoes to help soldiers in malaria-infected zones of the tropical Pacific.

The first and most famous of these insect-killing poisons was DDT, which stands for dichlorodiphenyltrichloroethane. In the 1940s, it was hailed as a miracle of modern chemistry. Spraying DDT on plant life could control malaria and typhus and other deadly diseases spread by insects. Crops and livestock could be protected from harmful insects. DDT was also used in home gardens. The United States Department of Agriculture and even universities that studied the program at first minimized the risks. This was a poison in the service of humankind.

Rachel Carson's influential 1962 book, *Silent Spring*, called for regulations to control the use of pesticides. DDT was clearly being overused—not only because of the harm it was doing to insects and other animal life, or because of the risks it posed to human health. It became apparent that the insects DDT was targeting were building up an immunity to it, making it increasingly less effective. More and more of it was needed to obtain the same results.

The fight over DDT was one of the major issues that led to the creation of the Environmental Protection Agency (EPA). The EPA banned DDT and has attempted to regulate the use of other dangerous chemicals, as well as control other practices that damage the environment.

Carson was one of the first to write about pesticides killing bees. She quoted a New York state beekeeper who said, "Up to 1953 I had regarded as gospel everything that emanated from the U.S. Department of Agriculture and the agricultural colleges." He was angry because in May 1953, after the state sprayed his area with DDT, 800 colonies of his bees died. The spraying had done so much damage to bees in the area that, when he sued the state for a quarter million dollars in damages, 14 other local beekeepers with similar stories joined his lawsuit.

Carson wrote of another farmer who lost 400 colonies after a 1957 spraying. The farmer said that every forager bee that was working in a heavily sprayed forest died and that half the foragers in a lightly sprayed field were also killed. Carson quoted him: "It is a very distressful thing, to walk into a yard in May and not hear a bee buzz."

Carson called her book *Silent Spring* because pesticides were killing the animals that made the sounds of spring that we love: birdsong and bee buzz.

The accidental killing of bees from pesticides continues. To compensate for bee losses, large government payments went to several states. Arizona was one of the biggest recipients: it lost half its bees between 1963 and 1977. Other pesticides were developed, but they only produced new forms of bee killing. Penncap-M had pollen-size grains that bees mistakenly stored in their legs and brought back to the hive, where the grains could poison the entire colony.

But this ongoing problem with pesticides did not explain why in 2004 there was this new and much larger wave of disappearing bees. Because pesticides were a familiar problem, they were among the first suspects. But bees killed by pesticides, and there have been plenty of them, leave behind carcasses. Hives were full of dead bees and dead foragers were found on the ground, hundreds or thousands of them in the field. But with CCD, the bees vanished without a trace. And this has happened in places where no pesticides were used.

Many thought CCD must be caused by some new pesticide that acted differently. The French thought they had found the answer. In 1994 the

chemical company Bayer had developed imidacloprid, an artificial nico-
tine. This was a new kind of pesticide, a neurotoxin that attacked an
insect's nervous system. This chemical was sold around the world, killing termites and protecting pets from fleas.

In France, it was also used to protect their sunflower crops. It worked
well and was widely used. It killed aphids, tiny vegetarian insects that eat
crops, as well as many other pests. But it also killed other animals, like
the valuable earthworm and several species of birds—and, according
to the EPA, who nevertheless did not ban it, it killed honeybees. They did
not document it causing bees to disappear.

The National Union of French Beekeepers said they had lost 1.5
million colonies in the beginning of this century, decimating the production of the South of France's celebrated honey. Bayer did research that
showed the pesticide had no effect on the pollination of forager bees.
Maybe so, but French tests showed that imidacloprid, which penetrates all
parts of treated plants, including pollen and nectar, can impair bee navi-
gation and affect their memory. Research in Italy also showed that the
pesticide could affect the bees' ability to use dance language. This was
what everyone had been looking for: a reason why bees could not find
their way home.

The French banned the pesticide, and between 2006 and 2007 the
death rate of bees in France dropped. For a moment, this new problem of
disappearing honeybees seemed to have been solved. But after a year,
bees were disappearing again, and the death rate of honeybees in France
started rising again. Some scientists do not think it is pesticides at all
but suspect one or several of the bee's natural enemies, like the *Varroa*
mite or the wax moth. That still leaves the questions of why these enemies are increasing and why bee resistance is decreasing. Also, most of
these enemies leave behind evidence of their work—such as stolen honey
or the white remains of bees killed by chalkbrood. None are likely to

leave an empty hive in good condition with full storages of honey and no dead bees. But viruses, like animals, mutate. They create alternative species, some of which fail and some of which prosper, and it is possible that a virus we do not know is acting on bees in a different way.

According to Darwin's law of natural selection, the mites who do a good job of picking their food will become more numerous and healthier, taking over the species. The best food choice for a mite is to eat a bee nursing a larva, a newborn bee. Recent research shows that *Varroa* mites are becoming more numerous and healthier.

It gets worse. In 1982 a new species of mite was discovered: *Tropilaelaps*, the parasite brood mite. This type of parasite was first identified on a honeybee in Sri Lanka. It has been plaguing the honeybee population in Asia, and logically would eventually move beyond that continent. Perhaps it already has.

Another suspect in this matter of the murdered bees has been genetically modified foods. These are crops that have been artificially altered to give them specific characteristics by taking genes from other organisms. The first genetically modified food was a slow-ripening tomato that was a commercial failure. But since then there have been tremendous successes with grains and other highly commercial crops. Many of these have been engineered to be insect resistant. Genes from bacteria that attack insects have been added into the plants' DNA.

Bacillus thuringiensis is a type of bacteria found in nature. In a natural application, it serves as a defense mechanism in the belly of caterpillars so that insect-eating insects do not harm these young animals. This bacteria was used to repel insects even before genetic manipulation became an available technique. The advantage of genetic engineering is that now it is not necessary to implant the bacteria. Genes from it are inserted into the gene pool of plants to create an insect-repelling crop, just as some caterpillars are insect-repelling by nature.

Crops with the genes of this bacteria can grow in huge fields free of insect predators, without the use of any chemicals or pesticides. But soon its consequences became clear: field after field of these crops also drove away good insects, like pollinator bees. Just like pesticides aimed at the insects we didn't want, genetically modified crops also killed some of the insects we wanted.

But there is a problem with this promising theory. Many countries, including most of those in Western Europe, refuse to plant genetically modified crops, and yet they still have a prevalence of CCD. Though there are many who strongly favor putting the blame on genetically modified crops, scientists remain skeptical. Research by scientists has yet to show a relationship between bee disappearance and genetically modified crops.

One theory holds that bees become disoriented by being trucked to a field to pollinate and then trucked to another across the country. According to this theory, this vagabond life stresses bees so much that they lose their limited ability to resist mites and diseases. However, there is no scientific research to support this.

CCD may be caused by a combination of these problems or even all of them. Or it could be the result of something that has not yet occurred to us. The fact that no cases of CCD have been reported among organic beekeepers is an intriguing clue. To be organic, the bees must live and pollinate in remote locations far from fields that have been sprayed with chemicals. Also, organic beekeepers do not use chemicals, whereas most commercial beekeepers use antibiotics against disease and pesticides aimed at mites. Organic beekeepers only let their bees feed on pollen and the honey that they produce themselves, while commercial beekeepers sometimes help out their bees with artificial feed—soy for pollen and high-fructose corn syrup (cornstarch that has been turned into fruit sugar) for honey.

Climate change may have caused some still-unknown consequences. Extremes in weather, which climate change is creating, are not good for bees. Rain, especially heavy downpours, keeps them from pollinating, forcing them to stay in the hive and not collect the nectar or pollen everyone needs. If it is extremely cold, pollen can become sterile, which means plants will not produce seeds. It also means the pollen lacks nutrients for bees. If the weather is very hot and dry, such as during many of the climate change–induced draughts in the western United States in recent years, flowers will not produce quantities of pollen or nectar. This leaves bees to go hungry. Warm weather also favors *Varroa* mites, which destroy bees.

And warm weather favors the Africanized "killer bees," with which honeybees cannot compete. They were first seen in the United States in Texas, and have spread throughout the Southwest, including parts of Southern California, and have also been found in Florida. But if the North American climate continues to warm up, these invasive bees might be able to settle as far north as Canada. Another bee-killer, the Asian giant hornet, so far limited to Asia, is experiencing growth and spread in its population, profiting from the warmer weather climate change has given us. The native Japanese honeybee knows how to fight off the giant hornet, luring a scout into the hive and then ganging up on it. But the Japanese and other Asians have brought in European honeybees because they are more productive honey producers, and these bees are defenseless against the large and aggressive giant hornet. If the hornets spread through climate change, this could be highly destructive to honeybee populations.

No workable alternative to natural pollination has been found. In the 1980s the excessive use of pesticides completely destroyed the honeybee population of the southern Sichuan Province in China, and the Chinese rescued their important pear crop by pollinating trees by hand. This is a very slow, labor-intensive process accomplished by extremely low-wage laborers. If Americans tried to rescue a crop by such a technique, the product would be way too expensive for most shoppers.

Scientists have been trying to get other species to pollinate and substitute for honeybees. While this probably would not produce honey, it might keep our crops alive. The problem is that most flowers are specialists, and only one pollinator can work with them.

Huge numbers of honeybees have vanished in this century, including about a third of all the honeybees in the United States. Because of all the crops that depend on them, bees are of tremendous economic importance. One study at Cornell University estimated that bee pollination contributes $15 billion each year to the US economy. While this is only a small fraction of the trillions of dollars in the US economy, it is a big enough loss that our government funds scientific programs to solve this problem. But we have yet to produce a solution.

Buried in shale in the Nevada desert is a cautionary tale. A fossil challenges the long-held belief that there was never a native American honeybee. This fossil is unmistakably a honeybee that lived in Nevada some 14 million years ago. It has been named *Apis nearctica* and it disappeared millennia ago. Exactly what happened, why it disappeared, is unknown.

PART THREE
BEETLES

12
MEET THE BEETLES

WHILE BEETLES AND BEES are among the most important pollinators, comparing their two pollinations is like comparing a classical music symphony to a rock concert. Beetle pollinations are wild and rough. Beetles do not have the sophistication of the fine-flying bees, with their dance communication and well-ordered society. At a beetle pollination, petals are chomped and sometimes defecated on, and the flower left behind is a mess.

The beetle does not gracefully lower herself onto the delicate landing petal but crawls in and is held there by the flower's petals, unable to leave for a day until the flower produces its pollen and the beetle is released. Happy to escape, it crawls over the pollen on its way out, becomes covered in it, and travels on to the next warm, irresistible-smelling flower. Many of the flowers that beetles pollinate—such as two popular

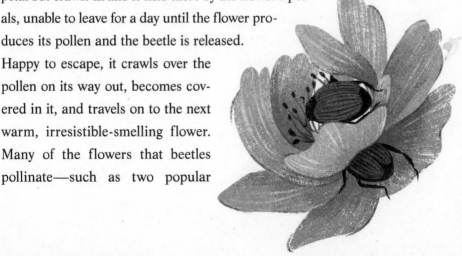

home garden plants, the *Dieffenbachia* and the *Philodendron*—put out heat and a scent to let the beetles know they are ready.

Coleoptera, more commonly known as beetles, is the largest insect order. Scientists have identified and named 350,000 species, but there are many more species to be found. The number of beetles in the world is not immediately obvious, because these insects come in so many different shapes and sizes. The smallest known beetle, found in Nicaragua, is only 0.325 millimeters, or slightly larger than a 1/100 of an inch. Goliath beetles in Africa can be more than four inches long. Another large beetle that lives in the Americas, the Hercules beetle, is thought to be the strongest animal on Earth because it can lift 850 times its own weight. That would be the equivalent of a 200-pound man lifting 85 tons.

Beetles, in all their varieties, pollinate many unusual and different flowers. Some think beetles may have been the first insects to pollinate flowers, millions of years ago. Beetles may have invented the idea.

Some beetles are thought to be hideous crawly pests and others charming. A few are considered valuable to the interests of humans. Because they come in such variety, beetles particularly fascinated Darwin. Wherever there was tremendous variation, as with orchids, Darwin could demonstrate evolution at work. But even before he developed his theory of evolution, he studied beetles. As a 19-year-old Cambridge student he began his lifelong interest in collecting beetles and identifying new species. In 2014 an American scientist examining Darwin's beetle collection from the London Natural History Museum noticed an odd specimen with an iridescent blue-green head and sawtooth antennae. He realized that the species had never been named and identified. It was a completely new genus, if you can call something that was first collected in 1832 new. Darwin had found it on the coast of Argentina during one of his famous voyages.

Indian culture has long valued beetles, with some wealthy collectors keeping prized samples in elaborate cages, and other enthusiasts using cardboard boxes with holes punched in the lid. In the 1950s, popular Indian writer Ruskin Bond wrote a short story called "The Big Race," in which boys released their prized beetles from their boxes onto a racecourse. Instinctively, the beetles ran, but the trick was to keep them running in the right direction to the finish line.

Despite their tremendous diversity, most of the hundreds of thousands of beetles have certain things in common. Many types of beetles go through holometabolous development, which means complete metamorphosis. Like some bees, most moths, butterflies, flies, and wasps, beetles are born from eggs that turn into larvae, which become pupae or cocoons, which hatch into adults.

Back in ancient Greece, Aristotle gave Coleoptera its name. He called it this because all beetles carry a shield (in Greek, a *cole*), which also serves as a wing (*ptera*). The shield is a hard outer part that protects the body. It is divided in two sections that can spread out like wings. Underneath and to the rear are two lightweight, fast-moving wings that accomplish takeoff, landing, and forward thrust by flapping. The two crescent-shaped shields are stationary when spread, and aid in lift like the wings on a glider. There are a few beetle genera that have no back wings and only the spreading shields. These beetles also can fly, but they do not fly very well.

One of the best-loved beetles is the ladybug. Many people throughout the world think that if a ladybug lands on them it will bring them good luck or good fortune. According to some, the amount of fortune depends on the number of dots on the ladybug.

The bug's popularity comes in part because ladybugs kill or drive away other insects we don't like. For this reason, they have long been a symbol of good luck. But also, they make us happy. They are round and pleasant looking, with bright and cheerful colors on their shields.

In English, "ladybug" was originally "ladybird," which meant a "bird of the Virgin Mary." In German it is called a *Marienkäfer,* which means a "Mary beetle."

In the Middle Ages, farmers, plagued by insects destroying their crops, prayed to the Virgin Mary. If ladybugs, which eat plant-eating insects, arrived to save the crops, they were thought to have been sent by the Virgin Mary, and so were called ladybugs or Mary bugs. Ladybug species come in different colors, but they always feature dots on a sharply contrasting background. Sometimes there are black dots on orange, red, or yellow; white dots on black; or dark blue dots on orange. There is always a minimum of 2 dots, sometimes 4 or 5, or maybe as many as 28. If there are an odd number of dots, one dot is often in the middle, split between the two sides. Sometimes a ladybug's whole shield is a checkerboard pattern. Some ladybugs change color with the seasons so that they continue to blend in with their surroundings. Since there are 5,000 known species of ladybugs, only slightly fewer than the total number of mammals, there are many varieties of patterns.

Ladybugs are hatched from bright yellow, bead-like eggs. Eggs take between four and eight days to hatch. Once they become larvae, which are sometimes brightly patterned but usually unattractive brown-and-yellow wormlike things, they become extremely hungry. The first thing they do is eat any other eggs that haven't yet hatched. But luckily, the mothers have produced extra unfertilized eggs just for that purpose. When the environment is stressed by climate or there are other factors making survival more difficult, the mother produces a higher percentage of these infertile eggs for food.

Some of the larvae then begin performing one of the ladybug's most appreciated services: they eat other small insects, such as aphids. Aphids are soft-bodied, well-camouflaged green creatures with mouths like pointed tubes that puncture plants and suck out their rich vegetable juices. If left alone, these little sap suckers destroy crops. Ladybugs also appreciate the nutritive value of green plant juice—but they let the aphids do all the hard work of eating the plants first, and then they gobble up the aphids' soft bodies with their strong beetle jaws. In some species, ladybug larvae can eat 500 aphids a day. The reason for this huge appetite is that this is the only stage in which the ladybug grows. The larva grows up to four times the egg size, forcing it to shed its hard outer shell for one four times bigger. Finally, after two to four weeks of gorging itself, the ladybug larva becomes a pupa. That's as big as it gets: it never grows again.

The defenseless pupa needs to retreat to safety during the process of transforming into an adult. Most insects do this by creating silk from the glue they secrete from the end of the abdomen. This silk is used to create a shell or cocoon. Sometimes the silk is simply the glue for a cocoon made of the insect's hair, wood, and other materials.

In cocoons, the pupa attaches itself to the leaves of plants. After 7 to 10 days, the adult insect chews its way out of the cocoon and emerges as an adult. Its shield is a pale yellow with no pattern at all. The newly emerged ladybug takes about 48 hours to develop its color and spots.

A ladybug lives about a year. The adult ladybug still manages to eat about 50 aphids a day, which, even allowing for the months of hibernation, means that a ladybug will about eat 5,000 aphids in its brief life.

Ladybugs have a smart and capable competitor. Ants do not so much want the aphids' plant juice, but they do love to lap up a sweet digestive juice put out by aphids, known as honeydew. When ants—the smart tough guys of the insect world, raised in a warrior culture—find lady-bugs eating their honeydew source, they try to drive them away by biting them with their sharp, powerful jaws. This is where we can easily under-stand the wisdom of the beetles' anatomical design. They tuck their legs under their completely flat bottom side and sit, exposing nothing but a hard-winged shell.

Ladybugs may not be fighters like ants, but they do know how to pro-tect themselves. Bright colors and bold patterns may be pleasing to humans, but in the insect world, and the animal world in general, they are usually a warning. Bright-colored frogs usually have toxic venom, and brightly colored snakes should be avoided. With insects, a bright color often means they have an unpleasant taste.

With ladybugs, the colorful patterns that attract us to them are also a memory aid to predators. Ladybugs are loaded with a cocktail of unpleas-ant chemicals that taste bad and make animals sick. They manufacture some of these chemicals themselves; others they store from various plants that they eat. Once an insect-eating animal—another insect, bird, or mammal—tastes a ladybug, they never want to eat one again. That bright polka-dot exterior is easy to remember. When predators see it, they stay away.

But many beetles do not have this nasty-tasting defense, nor do they have the bright colors of ladybugs. Darwin observed that many species of beetles have interesting colors: not as bright as ladybugs, but often with iridescent sheens. He concluded that this was for pleasing the opposite sex, noting that blind beetles living in dark caves do not have interesting colors, because they have no one they want to impress with their good looks.

Darwin wondered why some male beetles sported elaborate horns, which appear to be for fighting. However, no such battles were ever seen. And then there are some fighting beetles that don't have horns. Either way, it appears that male beetles make great efforts to show off for the opposite sex.

This was Darwin's most controversial theory, particularly in his native Victorian England, where the power of women was not an acceptable idea. Darwin believed that in addition to the selection made in evolution for survival, beetles and some other animals developed seemingly useless features that served no other purpose than to amuse and attract females—though, of course, attracting a mate is essential for the survival of a species. It has since been shown that this happens not only with beetles and certain other insects but also with some fish, mammals, and birds. It is the reason male birds are more colorful than female.

If the ladybug feels threatened, a small amount of yellow liquid will appear, dripping down the legs. This is the dreaded ladybug cocktail, which smells bad, tastes bad, and tells enemies to stay away. It is secreted in the beetle's blood and is called "reflex bleeding," because it is an automatic response to a sense of danger.

Ladybugs mate only with their own species. Scientists distinguish between species by the patterns on their backs, an unreliable technique because some species come in several patterns. But it is the best scientists can do, since they don't have the finely tuned smelling abilities of a ladybug. Ladybugs identify their own species and find their mates by smell, which they detect, like most insects, with their antennae.

The males, constantly looking for new partners, try through appearance and smell to seem attractive. They have to compete. But since the population is predominantly female, male ladybugs are in great demand.

One of their least charming attributes manifests itself when food becomes scarce. That's when ladybugs start eating other ladybugs, apparently indifferent to the unpleasant chemicals. Cannibalism is particularly common among our favorite ladybugs, those that eat aphids.

13
WHAT GOOD ARE THEY?

LONG BEFORE THE INVENTION of pesticides, pests that plagued agriculture were controlled with ladybugs.

While farmers prayed for ladybugs for centuries, actually taking them into fields to control aphids was first suggested in England in 1815. But ladybugs were not used, at least not on a large commercial level, until 1888, when they were brought to California from Australia to protect the orange crop from the cottony cushion scale, a visually descriptive name for a little, cushiony-looking white animal known as *Icerya purchasi*. Its large, fluted white cushions, not cottony to the touch, are actually the egg sac of a small, flat six-legged creature that feeds on trees, especially orange trees. These scales eat the leaves and the twigs, then the larger branches, and finally the trunk. They have no interest in the oranges themselves, but nevertheless they very efficiently destroy the grove.

In 1868 and 1869, acacia trees were brought to California from Australia. Too late it was learned that the acacia had brought with them the cottony cushion scale. The scale immediately found the orange groves.

Farmers chopped down infected trees to get rid of these pests, but the scales invaded everywhere there was citrus. Then, in 1888, Californians imported from Australia *Rodolia cardinalis*, commonly known as the vedalia beetle. This small ladybug, dark red with black spots, is also native to Australia, where they frequently live in acacia trees. Bright and sweet little animals to you, they are known to the cottony cushion scale as savage killers.

They also reproduce quickly. In the winter, 514 ladybugs were imported, and by June 12 the project had 10,555 to distribute to 208 citrus growers around California. By October, in the Los Angeles area, where the project had begun, there were healthy groves, and the cottony cushion scale had almost entirely vanished.

The original project cost $1,500, and by 1890, the California orange crop had grown enormously. A new approach to agriculture had begun. It was called biological control—forces within the natural order could be used to control unwanted populations. Descendants of the original 514 imported ladybugs were distributed around the world. Three descendants in Italy were the basis of a large population that protected the groves of France. Descendants in California went on to build colonies in Egypt, Cyprus, the Soviet Union, Portugal, Puerto Rico, Venezuela, Peru, Chile, Hawaii, the Philippines, Guam, Uruguay, Argentina, Taiwan, and Palau. Apparently, this ladybug can live, hunt, and reproduce in a wide variety of climates.

Biological control was the big thing in agriculture in the first half of the twentieth century. The convergent ladybug, or *Hippodamia convergens*, was part of a strategy to eliminate crop-destroying aphids. In wintertime, these ladybugs were commercially reproduced in mountain valleys and then packaged while hibernating, later sold to farmers in the spring. This was not always as spectacular a success as the original California projects. Even the merciless ladybugs aren't as good at killing aphids as they are at killing cottony cushion scale. With aphids reproducing much faster than ladybugs, it was hard for the ladybugs to keep up.

In the second half of the twentieth century, farmers lost confidence in biological control. This sophisticated and environmentally advanced approach was replaced with something far cruder. Farmers became captivated by new chemical controls: pesticides. But unintended consequences were just around the corner. Once DDT was used, the vedalia beetle population in the orchards of California's Central Valley almost completely disappeared, and guess who was back? The cottony cushion scale returned, killing some trees and stripping others of their leaves. Growers began paying as much as one dollar for each vedalia beetle.

But hard times were not over for the ladybug. Invading these California groves were thrips, little, skinny plant suckers with small wings for very limited flying. Vedalia beetles do not eat thrips, but growers could control them with a chemical called Baythroid. It was highly effective in killing a number of plant-eating insects, and its manufacturer, Yates, pointed out that this was

a low-level toxin, not nearly as deadly as DDT. Ladybugs would disagree. They found the chemical deadly.

The vedalia beetle is only one of many varieties of ladybugs disappearing. There are fewer and fewer ladybugs in the world, and if you pass

your summers enjoying nature, you may have noticed them missing. Even the nine-spotted ladybug, *Coccinella novemnotata*, is disappearing. The nine-spotted bug, which used to be the most common in the United States, has become extremely rare. Other native American species, such as the two-spotted ladybug and the transverse, are also becoming rare.

The nine-spotted ladybug is fairly big, with room for those nine spots. Once it was the most common ladybug throughout the Eastern Seaboard and the southern part of eastern Canada. Things changed in the 1980s. In most of this area, nine-spotted ladybugs have not been seen since the early 1990s. Since 1986, not one has been seen in Maryland. They disappeared from Pennsylvania in 1987, Delaware in 1988. Since the 1990s, studies have found few or none in many other states where they once made their homes.

Nine-spotted ladybugs are greatly missed, because they lived in many crops, including potato, alfalfa, corn, cotton, clover, and soybean—keeping them clear of aphids.

But one of the suspected culprits in their destruction, also an aphid eater, is the seven-spotted ladybug, brought from Europe.

While there has been extensive study of the disappearing bee problem, the investigation of the ladybug problem is far less advanced. A group at Cornell University has been studying it, asking amateurs—many of them kids—to record their observations. As with bees, there are more theories than answers.

A leading theory is that the introduction of nonnative species, such as the seven-spotted ladybug, has pushed out the natives. But this does not explain why these introduced species are doing poorly as well.

More species were introduced because ladybugs are very job specific. Different species favor certain parts of the plant as well as certain tasks, so it was thought that greater diversity might enhance their performance. Diversity is generally positive, but sometimes two species compete with each other for space or food. Large numbers of seven-spotted ladybugs were introduced from 1950 to 1970, and this corresponds to the beginning of the decline in native species. Another suspect is the Asian ladybug (*Harmonia axyridis*), which has regularly been introduced in many regions of the United States since the early twentieth century.

Lack of water may also be a problem. These animals require a watery environment, and due to climate change, certain regions, notably California, have become much drier.

And there is always the question of pesticides. The chemicals used to kill off undesirable pests may also be destroying desirable ones. There is irony in this, because the fewer ladybugs there are in the fields, the more farmers will turn to pesticides.

14
THE HEARTBREAKER

THE BEETLE THAT WILL break our heart if it vanishes from the planet is the firefly. It is unique. So much so that whole tourist industries have been built around it.

In Taiwan, more than 90,000 tourists take firefly-viewing tours every year. It is estimated that yearly, more than 80,000 tourists attend nighttime displays of fireflies in Malaysia. Every June, 30,000 people journey to the Great Smoky Mountains to see a nighttime display of fireflies. Those wild insects flying free in the night make the dark sky sparkle.

At first glance they are extremely ordinary to look at—certainly one of the least striking beetles. They belong to the family Lampyridae, with glimmering patterns of flashing light known as bioluminescence, light chemically produced in their lower abdomen. The telltale sign of its beetleness is its two sets of wings. The outer ones are hard and shaped like paddles, and the real working wings are tucked underneath. Like the ladybug, its outer wings fit together so tightly that when they are not in flight, they look like a single shell. But unlike a ladybug, the outer wing shell of a firefly is dull brown or grayish. Sometimes there are yellow, or even red, stripes. They are slender and flat. Like most insects, they have compound vision.

They have many names besides "firefly"—glowworms, lightning bugs, candle flies, firebugs. Most of these names are misleading. They are neither flies nor bugs. And not only are they *not* worms, but "glowworm" is also the name of a completely different insect with a similar lighting system. It gets confusing, but whatever they are called, they are much loved.

There are 2,000 known species of Lampyridae, and about half of them are found in North America. They live in marshes and climb on flowers both to suck nectar and to eat soft plant-eating insects. So fireflies draw admiring audiences for their light displays, and these insects are well appreciated by farmers. All 2,000 species have a common ancestor that lived 150 million years ago in the Jurassic age of the dinosaur, which makes the firefly a contemporary of the cockroach. The oldest Jurassic fireflies we have seen are stuck in amber from about 26 million years ago. Incredibly enough, the firefly of 26 million years ago looks much

Fireflies are the most famous example of bioluminescence. This may be because the intriguing patterns of their flashes make an extraordinary display right in front of us, or because their small bodies aren't visible, so we see only flashes of light moving enchantingly through the air. But bioluminescence is not rare in nature. It occurs in four of the five kingdoms and 11 phyla. It occurs in certain sea spiders, crustaceans, millipedes, centipedes, and even some flies. And that is just among arthropods.

Here's how these animals produce light: an enzyme, known as a luciferase, acts on a molecule, known as a luciferin. The physical reaction between the luciferase and the luciferin is always similar, but the chemical composition varies from one animal to another, producing a variety of colors of light. Scientists think the light process is a chance development. The chemically produced light in the abdomen of adult fireflies comes from cells called photocytes, or light cells. These are sandwiched between transparent outer cells, which serve as the lens, and inner cells behind them, which are filled with uric acid crystals and act as reflectors. The effect is like a naturally occurring flashlight.

Other animals evolved luminescence with different enzymes. Certain bacteria can produce a glow. At least 80 species of fungi glow an emerald green. There are numerous fish capable of bioluminescence, often deep-water species such as cookiecutter sharks, which use their light to attract prey. Anglerfish are not truly bioluminescent: rather than having their own chemicals, they dangle bioluminescent bacteria as bait for prey. Some 70 species of squid and some octopus have bioluminescence, as do numerous crustaceans, very small shrimp, and a few mussels.

like the firefly that dazzles us today. It is a fortunate thing that insects were attracted to plants with sap so that they could be trapped and perfectly preserved for us as the clear-tea-colored goo hardened to amber.

In evolution, genes get bad ideas and make mistakes. At the same time, good evolutionary ideas get passed on to more and more offspring. Some bad ideas work for a while and then die off while other good ideas become well established, which is what Darwin called "natural selection"—the natural process of promoting some variations and letting others disappear. A good idea is one that promotes the survival of the species.

We, *Homo sapiens,* are the only survivor of our genus, though there were various other species such as *Homo habilis,* the hairy *Australopithecus* and *Nakalipithecus.* These evolutionary relatives of ours have disappeared because they were not designed as well as we are. On the other hand, other members of our family from other genera, such as orangutans, gorillas, and chimpanzees, have, at least up until now, been successful. But it is a mistake to imagine that evolution moves in a straight line toward success. Because so many shoots and branches from our trunk have died off, we tend to think of evolution as a narrowing to a few advanced creatures.

Think of it as a hedge—something that grows more horizontally than vertically and is tight with gnarly branches, twigs, and shoots. Whole branches fail. We know from fossils that there are not only entire families, but entire phyla that have failed and vanished. But many shoots on the branches lead to success. That has happened in the insect world, which is why there are so many different kinds of insects. There is not a single evolved bug but many different insects with greatly different strategies. The web is so complicated that if it could start over again, it would never have similar results. This makes evolution seem as if it has moved forward by whimsy. Darwin rejected this idea. He believed that all the experimental changes (he called them variations) were for an evolutionary reason, even if we failed to understand what that reason was. Each variation was an answer to a specific problem.

Bioluminescence was a variation that proved a success.

It is difficult to understand why evolution turned to bioluminescence. Scientists think the luminescence in fireflies developed in the distant past, when a gene sequence was accidentally copied. This is called gene duplication, meaning there is an extra string of genes, one with no assignment and free to try out different things. One enzyme produced light, in what is called a mutation, or an uncalled-for change. But this change turned out to be a good one. Certain lines of fireflies had this ability and found that it worked well for courtship. Anything that works well for courtship succeeds, because reproduction is how a species survives. The fireflies that had this mutation reproduced abundantly and became dominant, and it became a standard feature.

Many, including Darwin, have been thrilled by the green luminescence of seawater at night when some of the tiniest of glowing creatures fill the tide, but nothing moves us as much as the flashes of thousands of fireflies on the summer night. It may be that we are somehow touched by their motives. Different animals use light to attract their victims; others use it as a warning. Fireflies light up the sky for love, or at least to find a mating partner.

The male firefly signals complicated patterns of light that seem to show off for their females but may have even more of a message. Different species have different codes: some long, slow burns; others quick flashes; some a combination; others, acrobatic light designs in flight. Fireflies are the only bioluminescent animal with a built-in switch to turn the light on and off in rapid sequences. We do not fully understand their code, but female fireflies do.

Only the males fly in search of a mate. The females respond only after a brief delay. The reason for this delay is not known, but it seems to vary from between one and four seconds, depending on air temperature. The female answers elaborate light patterns with single flashes. A dialogue is established between the male flash patterns and the single female responses.

The female light does not glow as brightly, so males have evolved bigger and better eyes. They know their own species by the light patterns. After some exchanges, they meet up and mate.

Firefly species in the eastern United States, famous for their light displays, are popularly called lightning bugs. One of the most popular is *Photinus pyralis*, commonly known as a Big Dipper lightning bug. A particularly large firefly, it lights up and dips toward the ground and then partially curves up, making a letter *J* in light. Seen primarily at dusk, they fly close to the ground, and they are comfortable in the backyards of suburbia. These are the ones that kids capture.

The leading European species is called glowworm fireflies. In this species, the females are wingless and shinny up trees to a prominent position. From there, they light up and remain glowing until they attract a male of their species. He flies but produces no light. It may take the female hours of glowing to attract a male. Some females also give off an enticing aroma to attract the opposite sex. In effect, they wear perfume. Almost a quarter of the fireflies in the world are the ones called glow-worms. They are common in all of Europe and much of Asia, but a rarity in North America. Male glowworms are not the only ones without lights. There are also so-called dark fireflies that fly in daylight rather than night. They find their mates entirely by smelling the scents emitted by the females without any lights.

Bioluminescence can turn up in various stages of a firefly's life. Sometimes even their eggs will glow, though why this happens is uncertain—perhaps it is to scare off egg-eating creatures. The one stage in which all firefly species glow is the larva, a stage that has nothing to do with mating—so scientists think the purpose must be a warning, a lure, or something to do with hunting. Like many insects, fireflies are their most brutal as larvae. At that stage, they need to take in as much food as they can in order to grow before they are sealed-up pupae. They devour animals that are much larger, such as snails and worms. They have sharp, powerful jaws and a small toothlike tube, through which they inject their victim with paralyzing poisons. We rarely see firefly larvae because they live underground or in water, where there are many animals to eat.

Larvae produce their glow from two spots at the end of their abdomen. If they are touched or in any way disturbed, they glow. Fireflies spend most of their lives as larvae before becoming pupae for two weeks, during which they continue to glow. At this stage, as they are transforming into adults, some species may have a completely different lighting mechanism than others. Some glow at this stage and never glow again.

Though the mating and the big light show seem like the exciting part of a firefly's life, when this occurs, the animal has only a few more weeks left to live. It is desperately trying to mate and pass on genes before it dies. The adult firefly does not even eat: it spends its stored energy until it dies.

The luminescence of fireflies also has commercial uses. Adenosine triphosphate, ATP, a molecule in all living things that is used to move chemical energy in living organisms, is a catalyst for making light in fireflies. Since the 1960s, food producers have been using luciferase and luciferin to test food. Since food is dead and ATP only appears in living organisms, the presence of ATP may indicate the presence of live bacteria. If, when placed on food, the firefly chemicals light up, that could be a warning that the food is contaminated. Furthermore, the more ATP, the brighter the light becomes. The firefly light is both a detecting and a measuring tool.

Since the 1990s, science has become much more sophisticated in using firefly material for research, particularly in the field of genetics. It also has had medical applications. Since luciferase lights up when in contact with ATP, and ATP is in all living things, luciferase can be used to detect life. It detects whether or not a cell is living, making it invaluable in medical research on cancer, tuberculosis, and other diseases. Conceivably, this technology could be brought to outer space to detect life on other planets.

Fireflies have many of the standard defense mechanisms of other beetles: bad odors, toxins, and reflex bleeding. They can smell particularly pungent when threatened, which some people have discovered when trying to capture them. In fact, fireflies make themselves so unappealing to predators that there is a long list of other animals with little defense other than that their appearance was designed to make enemies mistake them for the unappetizing firefly. Not only other beetles, but many unrelated insects, including certain moths and cockroaches, have adopted a striking similarity in appearance to fireflies.

This is a strategy in nature called Batesian mimicry, named after Henry Walter Bates, an English biologist and beetle enthusiast and collector, who discovered the role of mimicry. In a mid-nineteenth-century eleven-year exploration of the Amazon, Bates discovered there are many species that lack a defense system other than having evolved into a similar appearance to a species with a successful defense. Numerous insects have no defense other than their resemblance to a firefly. Most predators will pass them by, thinking that they taste terrible. Of course, an inexperienced predator may never have tasted a firefly and might not hesitate to eat the mimic, and will keep eating them until the day it stumbles across the real thing.

15
WHEN THE LiGHTS GO OUT

DESPITE THEIR MANY BIOLOGICAL strengths, firefly populations around the world are dramatically declining. One of their leading problems, as with many of the insects of the world, is that their natural habitat is being destroyed. They are grass dwellers but need water in all phases of their life—so they need to be near undisturbed grassy rivers, lakefront banks, or unexploited marshes.

Fireflies are not travelers. They cannot move to a better place if their habitat is destroyed. They live and mate where they are born, which means that their offspring do as well. This is a genetic design flaw. They were not designed for a world in which humans are constantly building. And firefly tourism—an industry based on people traveling to see fireflies—poses its own threats to the insects when an area becomes invaded by hotels, restaurants, and tens of thousands of tourists.

But tourism is not the only cause of destroyed habitat. A firefly tourist industry has grown in Malaysia, where the Selangor River runs to the sea, and in recent years, the firefly population has diminished. But the main problem is not the tourism. Anyone who had been to that section of the river and had known it from an earlier time would notice that the thick and tangled mangrove growth along the banks has been replaced by an oil palm plantation. On other parts of the river, mangrove trees were removed for shrimp farming. Both palm oil and farmed shrimp are important export products in the Malaysian economy. These spots became uninhabitable, and when the fireflies didn't move away to a new habitat, they died off.

In 2013, the Chinese imported 10,000 fireflies to a park in Shandong, hoping to create a tourist attraction. However, they had failed to grasp that central fact about fireflies: they don't move location. All the Shandong fireflies died.

And there's another type of pollution that you may never have even heard of injuring our planet: light pollution. If humans light up an area where there are fireflies, the females may go on bravely glowing, but the

males won't visit them. There will be no mating. Perhaps they are confused by the addition of artificial lights, or they find it hard to see. Given their inability to move elsewhere, that particular well-lit population will make no future generation and the population will die off.

It is not only fireflies whose vision is impaired by artificial lighting. In the 1960s, astronomers started complaining about light pollution, saying that it was impairing their ability to look into the heavens. Scientists researching light pollution have found that 80 percent of humans never see a truly dark sky. If you do have that rare occasion to see a night sky—in the Amazonian forest, northern Alaskan villages, Middle Eastern deserts—the sky is so dazzling a light show that you cannot stop looking up at it. Even if we accept living in a world where we never see true darkness, can never look up to see the night sky, the firefly cannot survive in such a place. It is also confusing for owls, turtles, frogs, and many other animals.

Another problem facing fireflies is that people like to collect them both for commercial purposes and for personal amusement. In America in the twentieth century, companies and research institutions that wanted luciferase paid children to capture fireflies.

In 1947 William David McElroy, a 30-year-old researcher at Johns Hopkins University in Baltimore, was working on solving the mystery of bioluminescence. He placed ads in newspapers offering children 25 cents for every 100 fireflies they brought to Mergenthaler Hall. There was also a 10-dollar bonus for the kid who brought in the most fireflies. In his first year, local kids brought him 40,000 fireflies, and 10-year-old Morgan Bucher Jr. won the 10-dollar prize.

More and more Baltimore kids got into the firefly trade, and there was little objection since McElroy was proving to be a pioneer of biotechnology—the application of new technologies to biology. But by the 1960s, when he was using up as many as a million fireflies a year, people started wondering about the wisdom of this huge harvest. The local newspaper, the *Evening Sun* wrote, "Life in Baltimore, for fireflies, became a chancy precious thing." McElroy assured the newspaper that only males were being taken and the females were left in the grass to lay their eggs. This may have been true, because the firefly population of Baltimore was never destroyed. But as research grew into a nationwide hunt for fireflies, it probably did contribute to a decline in the population.

In 1961, scientists at Johns Hopkins learned to make synthetic luciferin. But that made it even worse for fireflies. They were still necessary to make luciferase, and manufacturers needed a lot of them to keep up with the quantity of luciferin they could produce. Sigma, a St. Louis chemical company wishing to sell luciferase, advertised all over the country for firefly catchers, reaching out to Boy Scouts, science clubs, and church groups. They raised the price to 50 cents for 100 fireflies, with a $20 bonus for anyone catching more than 200,000. A concerned firefly expert, Sara Lewis, pointed to a woman in Iowa known as "Lightning Bug Lady," who shipped off a million fireflies a year, scooping them from a large net on her pickup truck. By 1979, the company was offering one dollar for a bag of one hundred, and in the 1980s, they were processing more than 3 million fireflies each year from around the country.

In 1985, scientists learned how to produce luciferase artificially, which stopped the wholesale slaughter. Now luciferin can be made without any firefly product at all. But there are still small companies that pay kids to bring in fireflies and sell their products. How much Sigma damaged the firefly population is unknown, but there are steady incidences of large-scale collecting of fireflies, and the practice is clearly endangering them.

And of course, as with all insects, they are threatened by pesticides.

The fact that real estate more than agriculture is encroaching on their habitat is not good news. Farmers are often targeted for their use of pesticides, but in reality, what people and businesses do with their lawns is often far worse. Farmers try to use pesticides that target particular insects that are damaging their crops. These pesticides do not always succeed and can result in unwanted poisonings. But home gardeners use pesticides that kill off almost everything. That includes fireflies. And if they survive, they will have nothing to eat. Remember, they cannot hunt elsewhere.

In the twentieth century, fireflies nearly disappeared from Japan.

Japan is a very good natural habitat for a number of fireflies, especially the ones that spend their larva stage underwater in the many rivers and streams and marshes of the Japanese islands. Even their wet rice fields are good habitat for fireflies.

Dating back to the seventeenth century, firefly catching was a popular children's sport. There is even a traditional song that Japanese children sing to the fireflies they are trying to catch. Fireflies are a frequent decoration on Japanese ceramics and are often in Japanese poems.

But in the twentieth century, the harmless children's sport became a commercial enterprise. Hunters would catch fireflies by the thousand at night and put them in little cages with wet grass to be sold in cities. Some were released in hotel courtyards and restaurants for customers to enjoy. But the tradition in Japan became too popular. As early as the 1940s, there were fewer fireflies. Further endangering them was the pollution of rivers from heavy industry. The insects' home was under siege by toxins.

The practice of capturing fireflies is not that unusual. In South America, wingless fireflies are called railroad worms because they have a red headlight and 11 green lights on each side of their long bodies. When people catch them, they keep them in a bamboo or clay cage, which is hung as a lantern. The fire-beetle of Panama, which is not a true firefly, produces so much light that a few in a jar provide enough light for reading. Some Panamanian women put these beetles in nets to decorate their hair.

With declining populations of their beloved firefly population, the Japanese took the initiative, reaping economic benefits along the way. There was still a tremendous commercial demand for fireflies, so the firefly hunters became breeders. They learned how to restore firefly populations with new breeding techniques. They learned what food larvae ate and even the right moss in which the females wanted to lay their eggs.

The Japanese truly became firefly experts. In the 1970s, when the fireflies began to even further decline, they understood exactly how to restore the insects' dwindling habitat. While the Japanese have been unable to restore fireflies' population to the large numbers they had before the twentieth century, they have brought them back significantly and are still able to enjoy impressive firefly festivals.

These days, fireflies are more than an old cultural symbol announcing the beginning of summer. They've become symbols of environmental rescue. We still can rescue the environment, bring it back, turn things around. That's certainly something to be proud of.

We need more such symbols of success.

Many beetles besides ladybugs and fireflies are disappearing. Maybe the modern world just isn't well suited for beetles. None of these others are as well-known or popular, but every species lost is a threat to others.

Among the endangered is the Ohlone tiger beetle. There are 2,000 species of tiger beetle, though only 100 in the United States. They have powerful jaws, are active hunters, and are much appreciated by farmers because they eat large quantities of small insects that feed on plants.

The Ohlone lives in Santa Cruz County, California, where homes and roads are increasingly replacing natural habitat. In the right environment, this little bright-turquoise beetle is ferocious. Because it was discovered only in Santa Cruz in 1987, the original range of this beetle is unknown. We do know this insect lives only in native grassland in clay soil. When there is construction on the grassland, the beetle is lost. It is also threatened by pesticides, which are abundant in the water runoff. Fields of crops are sprayed, it rains, and the chemicals end up in the water.

Another beetle threatened in this dangerous Santa Cruz environment is the Mount Hermon June beetle. These beetles live from one to four years but spend most of their time as larvae, living underground on roots. As adults, the females are too large to fly, but the smaller males fly close to the ground, searching for mates. They do this at night for about an hour; the rest of the time they are buried in the sand. They are called June bugs because they only come out in the summer. Both the building of homes and mining for sand have destroyed an estimated 60 percent of their habitat, and they are becoming extremely rare. Most of their habitat is privately owned and unprotected, although there is an attempt to purchase land for a protected reserve.

In Texas, the dryopid beetle was found in 1987 and first declared a new genus in 1992. Now it is already considered endangered. It lives in water but doesn't swim. At one time its range may have been wider, but now it lives only in the Comal Springs, natural freshwater springs in Texas. This beetle requires flowing, uncontaminated water.

Equally remarkable, a mold beetle that can survive only in caves of even temperature is known to remain in just two caves in Texas.

The American burying beetle is the state insect of Rhode Island. A striking black, orange, and red beetle, it lives off scavenging dead animals and is the rare beetle to show good parenting skills. The beetle was listed as an endangered species in 1989, but in 2015 the oil and gas industry in Oklahoma tried to have it removed from the list.

Protecting this endangered bug was interfering with business. The argument offered was that one little insect was a very small thing and an energy-producing industry was a very big thing. Think again. Saving the natural order—which means defending every species—is a very big thing, and the oil industry, which greatly contributes to climate change, may not be the best thing to preserve. The beetle remains on the endangered species list and is still protected.

This beetle used to live in 35 states and 3 Canadian provinces but is now reduced to only 5 states and Ontario. Though pesticides are blamed, it is also pointed out that this beetle began to disappear even before the invention of DDT. The birds and wild mammals that provided this beetle with food have been vanishing, and this may be the main problem.

Biologists have been trying to prevent extinction by releasing laboratory-raised American burying beetles, creating a beetle population on Penikese Island and Nantucket in Massachusetts. Biologists return each year to both islands to study the survival and growth of the beetle population. The hope is that such studies can find a way back for endangered species.

PART FOUR

BUTTERFLIES

16

BEAUTiFUL
LEPiDOPTERA

WE TEND TO THINK of butterflies as more important than moths. This shows how much our grasp of the natural order is based on our emotions. More than other species, we humans tend to side with whomever or whatever we find beautiful. Lepidoptera—which we think of as the butterfly order—actually has 10 times as many moth species as butterflies. In evolution, butterflies were a later arrival. They actually evolved from moths. Moths pollinate in the dark of night, so nature saw no reason to dress them up in bright colors. After all, few would see them in the dark.

In fact, there are a few daytime moths, and these are more colorful. Butterflies pollinate by day, when they can be seen. With their patterns and colors, they do not disappoint.

There are more types of butterflies than birds—about 15,000 species of butterfly compared to 9,000 bird species. Don't forget, of course, that these are only the ones discovered so far. Clearly, there are more individual butterflies than individual birds flying around the world. This follows a rule of nature that is not always true but is generally reliable: the smaller the animal, the more individuals. In other words, even in a healthy ecosystem, there would be a lot of ants and not many elephants.

This variety of species of butterflies has adapted to many climates. They are found in the arctic, in deserts, in temperate forests, and in grasslands. The largest concentrations are in tropical rain forests. That is because butterflies like water and heat. In more northerly climates, a butterfly, for example a monarch, while summering up north, will sit in the sunlight with its wings spread to absorb heat. Desert butterflies hide under rocks in midday and come out when the sun is setting. At that time of day, they can be found drinking at water holes.

It is guessed that about two-thirds of the butterflies in the world live in tropical rain forests. Since thousands have still not been identified, scientists cannot provide an exact number. So far, 2,000 species have been found in the Brazilian rain forests alone.

Butterflies are another example of the rich choices of evolution. They have survived by evolving into many sizes and shapes. The largest butterfly is the Queen Alexandra's birdwing butterfly with its 11-inch wingspan. But some butterflies have a wingspan of an inch or less.

We love butterflies for their beautiful patterns and colors and the many different varieties. That is why people collect them. But nature does not create beauty for our enjoyment. A few species of butterflies are beautiful to attract females. A female Queen Alexandra's birdwing butterfly is a plain brownish pattern, but the male, in order to attract her, is a lovely sky-blue, mauve, and indigo pattern.

Often the look of the wings is determined by the climate in which butterflies live. Cold-weather butterflies tend to be dark, because dark colors quickly absorb heat. Butterflies that live in hot places tend to have light-colored wings to deflect heat—just like how people wear dark clothes in the winter and light-colored clothes in summer.

Butterfly wings offer numerous other survival strategies. Butterflies often have round spot patterns. They are designed to look like eyes—not compound insect eyes but an eye with a single pupil that is characteristic of mammals. The owl butterfly has wings that resemble the face of an owl. Even stranger, the wings of the death's-head hawk moth appear as a macabre face mask.

Sometimes these patterns are designed to scare off predators. Often they are designed to attract them so that the bird pecks at the wings, causing minor injuries rather than a fatal jab to the body. The outer border of the monarch wing is black with white spots, exactly like the body in the center, to fool birds into harmlessly jabbing the edges.When Europeans came to North America and first saw butterflies, the colors reminded them of the black-and-orange banner of Prince William of Orange, who became King William III of England. That's how the monarch butterfly got its royal name.

Like ladybugs, monarchs taste bad. Birds that eat monarchs that feed on milkweed become poisoned with a substance called cardenolide. Once that bird recovers, it never wants to taste a monarch again. The bright colors that we find attractive are actually a warning sign for predators. Once they eat a nasty-tasting butterfly, predators remember the color and stay away.

As with the fireflies, here we find another example of Batesian mimicry. In areas where there are monarch butterflies, there are other butterflies that resemble them, such as the viceroy butterfly and the queen butterfly. These butterflies don't taste like monarchs and are a perfectly delicious meal for predator birds. However, hungry birds pass them right by. A viceroy butterfly is so named because in the rules of royalty, a viceroy is an official who stands in for a monarch.

Darwin admired the work of Bates as an illustration of how evolution works. The viceroy does not one day decide to dress up as a monarch. They have to have some similarity to begin with—probably size and shape. A similarly sized but defenseless butterfly might develop a spot or two similar to a toxic butterfly in the area. If that results in predators avoiding them as they do the toxic neighbor, they will, in following generations, acquire more similar markings until eventually they resemble their toxic neighbor so closely that they are rarely attacked.

Batesian mimicry is good for the imitators but not for the imitated. It encourages predators to attack. After a number of good experiences preying on viceroys, a bird will unknowingly sample a monarch. The monarch and other imitated butterflies will slowly evolve into a slightly different pattern. A stripe will be added or a spot removed. And if butterflies with this variation are not attacked, the altered butterfly will become standard in later generations.

The inherent natural struggle for survival makes the butterflies' chemistry perform in this way. If enough birds mistakenly sample the toxic butterfly, they will find a way around the toxin. Some birds have learned how to attack a monarch, identify the poisonous parts, and then eat around them. In order to survive, the butterfly's body must keep innovating.

Butterflies have many forms of mimicry, copying everything from bird poop to plant leaves, often with impressive detail. Vladimir Nabokov, the famous Russian American novelist and recognized authority on butterflies, described various forms with great excitement:

> When a certain moth resembles a certain wasp in shape
> and color, it also walks and moves its antennae in a
> waspish, unmothlike manner. When a butterfly has to
> look like a leaf, not only are all the details of the leaf
> beautifully rendered but markings mimicking grub-bored
> holes are generously thrown in.

Another European biologist working in the Amazon, Fritz Müller, discovered that some species had found an even better solution, which was named after him and is now known as Müllerian mimicry.

With Müllerian mimicry, the mimics not only evolve into the look of the poisonous one, they also develop the poison. In these cases, a predator is sickened no matter which species it samples, and predators learn to avoid anything with that appearance.

It is not surprising that monarchs have a tough time surviving. The more specific an animal's needs are for survival, the less the chance they will make it. The great weakness of monarchs is that they need milkweed bushes in order to reproduce. Milkweed is the only food that monarch larvae eat. A responsible mother monarch would not lay her eggs anywhere else, because otherwise her offspring would starve. She lays her eggs on milkweed because she knows that once the larvae hatch, they will have to eat something. The egg is a barely visible dot stuck on the back of a milkweed plant leaf. Each larva has its own plant.

The larva—or caterpillar—must eat. It grows to many times its original size in 9 to 14 days before it moves on to the next stage. Unfortunately for caterpillars, wasps do not seem to mind the monarch's toxic taste. The wasps themselves are desperate to feed their own hungry larvae. That helps explain why there are so many larvae: it is another law of nature that the greater the chance that a species' young will be killed, the more offspring are produced.

The odds are against any butterfly. As a caterpillar, they shed their skin at least four times while growing. Between lack of food; natural enemies like ants and wasps; pesticides; and not to mention viruses and bacteria, many larvae die without ever nestling into the safety of a cocoon. They are highly visible with their bright yellow color and black-and-white bands. They also have a pair of antenna-like tentacles on both their head and tail, which makes it difficult for a predator to know which direction a monarch caterpillar is facing and to distinguish between its front and back.

The butterfly caterpillar does not form a cocoon as do other insect larva. Other insects squirt some gluey silk and gather it with additional available materials to form a cocoon, a hard shell in which to live. But the butterfly caterpillar lets out a small amount of silk to glue itself to an appropriate spot on the milkweeds, hanging in the shape of the letter *J*. Then its outer skin hardens to a durable shell known as a chrysalis. The chrysalis is an impressive casing. It is a rich green color with one black band studded with metallic gold shards. There are also a few golden pieces that look randomly placed. From the outside, the chrysalis hanging from a leaf by a thread of silk looks lifeless. But a lot is happening inside. Their bodies are constantly changing—what must be a very strange experience. The body digests itself and breaks down to what seems a gooey soup of cells. But then these cells organize themselves to form the different body part. The last thing to occur before fully transforming into an adult monarch butterfly is gaining the signature white, black, and orange pigments on the wings. It is time to break out of the chrysalis and begin life as a butterfly.

17
THE INCREDIBLE JOURNEY

MONARCHS MAY NOT MAKE honey or flash light shows in the night, but they are useful pollinators. By the mouth is a curled-up sucking tube called a proboscis that they can unfold to reach deep into the well or long tube of flowers that have evolved for butterfly pollination. Different butterflies have different proboscises to fit with the flower that they pollinate. Moths have even more variety. In Madagascar the hawk moth unfurls a foot-long proboscis to just fit in the tube of the particular orchid it is designed to pollinate.

For whatever reason, to us, monarchs are beautiful. But maybe the reason we so love them is that their story is incredible.

Monarchs belong to a family of butterflies, most of them orange, that in the larva stage live on milkweed. The scientific name is Danaidae, but this family is usually called milkweed butterflies. All Danaidae are tropical animals, but only the monarch chooses to spend part of its life in a temperate zone.

Being a tropical animal, it cannot survive the winter temperatures of the north. Every winter, the monarch migrates south to stay warm. In the spring, they return to their northern ground, where they mate. No other butterfly has such a spectacular migration, flying 2,000 to 3,000 miles each way.

Once they become adult butterflies, they can mate several times over the course of their lives. They no longer eat anything but nectar and are drawn to asters and goldenrod, marigold, zinnia, cosmos, and sunflowers.

Monarchs use energy from the sugar-rich nectar to fly south. They are great fliers. They do not fly swiftly in powerful strokes. You do not see them fluttering and flapping when they are migrating. They have unusually large wings, which they spread to catch warm air currents rising in the sky, and they glide, not traveling swiftly but saving energy like a glider plane not using an engine. Sometimes winds blow them off course, but they seem to know how to correct these errors.

Butterflies start flying not long after sunrise and continue only until the early evening. They, like bees, seem to have a good sense of time. They need visible landmarks by which to navigate, and they also use the sun. At night, they rest. If they accidentally find themselves over water at nightfall, they must find a place to perch. Yet they do manage to navigate from an altitude of more than 1,000 feet on a cloudy day. That is because they have in their thorax tiny pieces of magnetite, a magnetic iron ore. This creates a kind of built-in compass. Magnetism tells them the location of the magnetic north, by which they can calculate any direction.

Their migration is a slow process. It can take two months to get to their winter grounds. The monarch can accomplish this long voyage because it lives longer than other butterflies, as long as nine months as a butterfly. By insect standards, this is a very long and full life. The Indian poet Rabindranath Tagore wrote:

The butterfly counts not months but moments,
and has time enough.

Many butterflies have north-south migrations, including painted ladies, which are believed to be the most common butterfly in the world. None migrate as far. Some barely move at all. Florida monarchs do not migrate. The Colorado hairstreak moves only a few yards in its entire life. In past centuries, when there were more butterflies, there may have been more and larger migrations. There are records from earlier times of the sky suddenly filling with butterflies. On July 9, 1508, it was recorded that in Calais on the north coast of France, the sky became so thick with white butterflies "coming out of the northeast and flying south-eastwards, so thick as flakes of snow" that men in the fields outside of town could not see the town at four in the afternoon.

The exact migration of the monarch was not discovered until 1976, when two Canadian zoologists, Fred Urquhart and his wife, Nora Patterson, traced them to their winter home. It was previously observed that monarchs were present in North America during the spring and summer, but they vanished in the fall and winter. Some people had believed that they hibernated through the winter in hollow trees. Others thought that they migrated, but couldn't imagine them going farther than the warm weather of Florida. But there were no influx of monarchs into Florida in the winter.

In the 1940s, Fred and Nora struggled to invent a tag that could be stuck to a fragile butterfly wing without damaging or impairing it. This is an exceedingly difficult task. Tagging a butterfly requires an extremely small and delicate tag, and extremely delicate handwork. But they learned how to do it, so that later, if the dead butterfly was found, it had a tag that read, "Send to Zoology University of Toronto Canada."

They founded a network of thousands of volunteers to tag butterflies. By 1975, they had tracked the winter monarchs to the rugged mountains east of Mexico City. After two years of searching, two biologists, Catalina Aguado and her husband, Ken Brugger, followed the monarchs to a forested area of the Cerro Pelon in the mountains of the Mexican state of Michoacán. They came across an astounding sight in the woods: wave after wave of orange, an orange-and-white forest. Some trees were completely covered with butterflies. Sometimes the air looked like an orange blizzard was sweeping in. There were so many that when a group took to flight, the rustling of flapping wings could be heard.

At one time this place had been a volcanic area. Then it became a cold-weather evergreen forest. Because it was high in the mountains, the cold-weather forest remained. Its 150-feet-high oyamel fir trees are magnificent to look at and favored by monarchs.

On January 9, 1976, Fred Urquhart found on the forest floor, among the many millions, a butterfly with his tag. It had been placed on the butterfly by two schoolboys from Chaska, Minnesota, in early August 1975. The migration was proven. Catalina Aguado posed on the cover of *National Geographic* magazine, covered in orange, white, and black monarchs.

The monarch butterflies that spend their summers east of the Rocky Mountains move to Central Mexico when the weather turns cold. Those that summer in the west only migrate to California for the winter. But scientists are not sure how many winter destinations monarchs have. There seems to be another one for western butterflies, traveling through

Arizona to the Sonoran Desert of Mexico. Some think all the western monarchs are California residents—some of whom spread out in the summer and keep returning to California, while others reside permanently in California. In Australia, the monarchs seem to migrate between inland and coastal areas. Nowhere else has a monarch migration been found, and nowhere has any insect migration been discovered on the scale of the one from the Northeast to Central Mexico.

In California, about some 400 sites along the coast and down into the Baja California coast of Mexico have been discovered. None approach the size of the Michoacán gathering places. Some sites have fewer than 20 butterflies and some have 100,000.

But monarchs are not the only ones who like these spots near the California coast. People like them too. Some wintering sites have been lost to real estate projects. The good news is that in 1988, California voters approved a bond that bought and protected some of these sites. Also, agreements have been made with some property owners not to disturb monarch areas on their property.

Until the mid-nineteenth century, monarchs were thought to be a uniquely North American species. Then, in 1840, they were seen in New Zealand. And in the Atlantic they were seen in the Canary Islands in 1860, and Azores in 1864. They have also been sighted in Hawaii. In 1876, one was found in Wales, and several others were sighted in the next month in other parts of southern England. The following year, one was sighted on the Atlantic coast of France. At the time, it was not even known that insects migrated. It was not until 1980 that monarchs were found in Spain, and it is now established that there is a colony that lives, reproduces, and migrates there. They seem to have migrated from there to North Africa. In recent years, monarchs have become a familiar sight on the Cornish coast, the part of England closest to North America.

At the same time, in the mid-nineteenth century, monarchs seem to have journeyed across both the Atlantic and the Pacific. At first it was thought they accidentally hitched rides on ships. But monarchs were too numerous for that. Many of these areas at this time started developing native milkweed. Do monarchs have far greater flying skill than we have imagined? It is already known that monarchs are perhaps the most skilled fliers of all insects. It remains a mystery how these butterflies that fly by day and rest at night have been crossing the oceans. They appear to have arrived in large numbers in certain years. Of the 450 monarchs that were recorded in Britain between 1876 and 1988, more than three-quarters of them arrived in two different years, 1958 and 1981. But the migration appears to be increasing, with large numbers seen every year since 1995.

Monarchs have also established themselves on Caribbean islands and in northern South America. These small colonies are older than those in Europe and the Pacific. But none of these newer colonies have a population comparable to North America, where their survival is essential to the continuation of the species.

For the survival of the North American monarch, it is critical that the oyamel fir forest of Michoacán be saved. The forest has already been reduced to its last 100,000 acres. The locals own the land but are not allowed to sell it. They are very poor and do what they have to in order to survive. They sell the valuable oyamel lumber and farm the cleared land. The trees are often used to build homes or are even burned for fuel.

The Mexican government created the Monarch Butterfly Special Biosphere Reserve in 1986. This has not stopped the local farmers from cutting down trees; it has simply made the practice illegal. At the time of its 1976 discovery, there were 1 billion monarchs in Michoacán. Today that number is closer to 500 million.

The problem was that the government gave the locals no economic incentive to cooperate. In recent years, realizing their mistake, the Mexican government has tried to couple protection of the butterfly forest with economic programs that provide alternatives to logging. Locals are now earning some money from butterfly tourism, hired as guides for visitors who want to see the butterflies, and selling T-shirts and souvenirs. This gives them an economic interest in preserving the butterflies. There are many times when in order to help the environment, you first have to help people.

18
SURVIVING A CHANGING WORLD

SINCE THE MONARCH'S LIFE cycle is all about climate, changes in temperature, and the shifting of seasons, it is clear that climate change is going to have profound impact on this butterfly. It is uncertain what the monarchs' future will be. Warmer winters might help monarchs, but hotter summers might mean that their summer homes could become too hot for survival. The trend toward droughts is also a threat because butterflies need water. Extreme heat and a lack of water are also threats to the milkweed plants, essential for the reproduction of monarchs.

Milkweed only flourishes in moderate climates and is damaged by extreme cold or extreme heat. So milkweed and, consequently, monarchs need a temperate climate.

A notable increase in draught conditions in Texas, an important stopover for migrators, has already caused a decline in the monarch population. Heavy rainfalls have also been causing deaths of monarchs.

Monarchs cannot survive cold weather, which is why they migrate. They can survive freezing temperatures, but if the temperature drops below 17 degrees, monarchs will die.

Here is some really bad news for North American monarchs: it is predicted that by the year 2030, the area suitable for oyamel firs in Mexico will have declined by 70 percent because of climate change. If climate trends continue, there will be almost none of these trees left by 2090. This would be the end of the world's largest monarch population.

Even if enough of the necessary habitat survives, milkweed in the north and oyamels in the south, the monarchs take temperature as clues to when to head north and when to migrate south—so a change in climate could cause complete confusion in their life cycle. They might, for example, head north too soon or stay north too late and then freeze to death.

Temperature also gives signals for when to reproduce, and some studies have already suggested declining populations due to climate change have caused monarchs to reproduce less.

Another newer problem for monarchs might be genetically modified organisms (GMO). As with most GMO issues, the connection is not certain, but studies do show that between 1999 and 2012, while two GMO products, Bt corn and glyphosate-tolerant crops, became widespread in the Midwest, milkweed declined 64 percent in the region. Monarchs—without milkweed for their eggs and to feed their larvae—declined 88 percent.

Some soy and later some corn became genetically engineered to be able to withstand a deadly herbicide called glyphosate. That meant that glyphosate could be used to kill off weeds without harming the GMO grains, which were branded Roundup Ready. Because of the planting of Roundup Ready grains, farmers were free to kill off soil-robbing weeds with heavy doses of glyphosate without endangering their crops. According to the US Department of Agriculture, the use of glyphosate in soybean fields rose from almost 44 million pounds in 1995 to over 122 million pounds in 2014. On cornfields it went from 4.4 million pounds in 2000 to 63 million in 2011.

This has resulted in a decline in milkweed—and a decline in monarchs. Milkweed is officially classified as a weed. Weeds are plants that have no use and offer no beauty. Of course a "weed" is often a personal judgment. To a farmer, a milkweed is a weed. But milkweed is vital for the life of the monarch butterfly, and the monarch might even pollinate a plant the farmer likes. It is an example of why, in nature, before killing off something considered "undesirable," the consequences to the natural order have to be considered.

19
AN UNBROKEN DANCE

ASIDE FROM THE DAMAGE to the natural order from the lose of butterflies, their absence would be a sad blow to a large number of people.

Nabokov, an important butterfly expert with a genus and several species named after him, wrote, "It is astounding how little the ordinary person notices butterflies." This is not really true. Perhaps we don't write 22 scientific papers on the subject or discover new species, as he did, but we do notice. Butterflies thrill us with both their beauty and the seemingly whimsical lifts and turns of their fluttery flight. They always have. Tu Fu, the celebrated classical Chinese poet of the eighth century, wrote:

And butterflies linger playfully—an unbroken
Dance floating to songs orioles sing at their ease.

A much earlier mystic, Zhuang Zhou, one of the fourth-century BCE founders of the religion known as Taoism, wrote that he had a dream that he was a butterfly. When he awoke, he saw that he was a man. But how did he know that he wasn't still a butterfly just dreaming that he was a man?

In many cultures through the centuries, butterflies have provoked such mystical thinking. Ancient people throughout the world drew images of butterflies.

The ancient belief of Hinduism, the world's oldest practicing religion, that all living things keep returning to a new life is often said to have come from observing the metamorphosis of butterflies. The ancient Egyptians had a similar device, but they took it from observing the metamorphosis of beetles rather than butterflies. Still, the Egyptians associated butterflies with the dead, and painted butterflies on the walls of their tombs. The ancient Greeks used the same word for both "soul" and "butterfly": "psyche." In 1500 BCE, the Mycenae civilization in southern Greece made beads that represented butterfly cocoons. A tile mosaic floor in the Roman city of Pompeii buried by a volcano eruption in the first century AD shows a butterfly emerging from a skull, the soul rising from the dead. In Japan, a white butterfly is a soul about to depart for another world. Kobayashi Issa, the eighteenth-century master of haiku, a Japanese style of verse only 17 syllables long, wrote:

The flying butterfly, I feel myself a creature of dust

In the Northwest, some Blackfoot women make a beaded butterfly on deerskin and tie it into a child's hair to help the child sleep.

In the lore of both the Mayans of Central America and the Irish, butterflies are the souls of the recently departed, searching for their place. Aztec warriors went into battle with a butterfly on their shields. A 1680 Irish law banned the killing of white butterflies because they were thought to be the souls of children.

But butterflies do not always have a positive image. In Scotland and other Northern European cultures, butterflies were believed to be the souls of witches. In the Middle Ages and for centuries later, it was believed that butterflies were fairies in disguise. Their mission, it was often agreed, was to steal milk and butter. That is the origin of the English language word "butterfly." In Spanish it is called a *mariposa*, a landing of the Virgin Mary.

Later, in the eighteenth century, Europeans, especially the English, became enthralled with their collections of butterflies captured, killed, and fixed with a pin. In England, such butterfly enthusiasts were called aurelians, a name referring to certain golden-colored butterfly cocoons.

Biology, and especially the study of insects, in the eighteenth and nineteenth centuries, relied on amateurs. Even Darwin was able to pursue his interests because he came from a wealthy family. The natural sciences were very fashionable in nineteenth-century Europe and America, and a glass cabinet displaying rock and insect collections was a common feature in household living rooms. Butterflies were the most common display.

Before the twentieth century, the countryside was aflutter with far more butterflies than we see today. There were no chemical fertilizers and no insecticides, fewer and more narrow roads, fewer homes, and no shopping malls. Agricultural fields were smaller and were surrounded by thick, high hedges that marked the borders of fields and were havens for butterflies and other insects. There were also more ponds and marshlands. More unmowed pastures full of wildflowers. The air was filled with butterflies, and people enjoyed collecting them.

In England it was a pastime of rich and poor, artists, writers, and politicians, including numerous prime ministers. And at a time when many pursuits were exclusively male activities, women were also aurelians.

One of the earliest and best-known female aurelians was Eleanor Glanville, who was born in England in 1654, before the word "aurelian" was invented. Although not an aristocrat, she was wealthy, and when she died in 1709, she upset her son by leaving all her money to a cousin instead of him. He went to court and claimed that she had been out of her mind. One hundred witnesses, mostly local villagers, were questioned. They were full of stories of how Eleanor used to run through the fields with a net, capturing butterflies. Since the constricting corsets and long, heavy skirts worn by seventeenth-century women were too cumbersome for this kind of activity, she had been seen in various states of undress, though probably no one today would think this. It was enough to convince the court, and the son was awarded the inheritance.

But in later centuries, butterfly collecting became very acceptable behavior. There were many odd things about Walter Rothschild of the wealthy banking family, born in 1868. He showed no interest in the family banking. He rode through London in a carriage drawn by zebras. But no one thought his butterfly collecting was odd. In his 69-year lifetime, he collected 2.25 million butterflies and moths, which he left upon his death in 1937 to the British Museum. He did not find most of them but hired "professional collectors," romantic adventurers who traveled to all corners of the Earth armed with a pistol and a net.

Butterfly collecting remained a passion. Nabokov was the most famous collector of the twentieth century. Butterflies and butterfly collecting constantly appear in his novels, short stories, and poems. Like Darwin, as a young man he had developed a passion for insects. He wrote in his autobiography, "Few things indeed have I known in the way of emotion or appetite, ambition or achievement, that could surpass in richness and strength the excitement of entomological exploration." He said that writing and butterfly collecting were his two greatest pleasures in life.

A butterfly collector was essentially an amateur scientist, and the ultimate goal was to find, identify, and name a new species. Nabokov, who accomplished this numerous times, maintained that this, more than his famous novels, was his one enduring accomplishment.

But butterfly enthusiasts have become part of the problem.

20
THE DANGEROUS NET

MANY MORE BUTTERFLIES THAN just the monarch are in trouble. Their colorful beauty was designed to be their protection, but what scares off other predators attracts humans. Butterflies, in addition to all the other plagues that insects face, are the victims of collectors. The more beautiful they are, the more they are endangered by collectors. Aurelians can be a menace.

Nature did not foresee the butterfly net. Females fly more slowly than males, so most of the butterflies caught by collectors are female. It would be better to catch males, because there are many more of them.

The individual male is not as valuable as the female to the reproduction of the species.

It is not certain how much of a threat butterfly collectors represent today. In past centuries, when a collector would think nothing of grabbing a hundred samples of a species to provide to various collections, collectors were a considerable threat. Only rarely would someone suggest that too many of a particular species were being taken, as in the early 1800s, when scientists suggested that too many Adonis blues were being taken in England. Certainly, collectors never caused as much harm as the loss of habitat. But occasionally still, there is a rare butterfly, highly valued by collectors, that is taken by locals and sold as a souvenir, harming the population. A butterfly of Central and South America, the blue morpho—described by Nabokov as "so ample and radiant that they cast an azure reflection upon one's hand"—is threatened because its brilliant iridescent-blue wings are used to make jewelry. But this threat is not nearly as severe as the rapid destruction of its habitat: tropical rain forests.

There are as many—or more—butterfly enthusiasts today as ever. But now only a minority kills the butterflies. In the mid-twentieth century, Nabokov was still collecting tens of thousands of specimens. Such collectors identified them and recorded their findings in the same tradition as bird-watching. But birds are not killed and pinned to a board. Today, often butterflies are not either. Many like to photograph butterflies, and the camera has replaced the pinboard.

Thirty-three butterflies are on the endangered species list. The Fender's blue butterfly and a close relative, the Mission blue butterfly, are on the list. These are beautiful animals, not loud and bright like monarchs, but a most delicate shade of pale blue with a fine lacy pattern. These butterflies live along the coasts of Oregon and California, eating and laying eggs in the lupine. The lupine flowers shoot straight up out of coastal grassland in purple or other bright colors. Once again, the problem is that this coastline is valuable real estate, so there is less and less wild grassland and fewer lupines. That means fewer butterflies. Since the butterflies pollinate the lupine, that makes fewer lupine still. They are caught in a downward spiral.

In Florida the once common atala hairstreak butterfly is struggling. For food it relies on cycads, thick-trunked, spiky-leafed plants that are pollinated by beetles. So this is a case of a butterfly that depends on a beetle. The striking black, turquoise, and orange butterfly, like most colorful insects, is poisonous, in this case from a toxin derived from eating cycads. People had little use for this plant and started chopping it down as they built homes. By the late 1950s, this butterfly was thought to be extinct.

But here is one of the rare cases of an insect saved by the suburbs. The landscapers who designed homes and communities and parks decided that cycads were an attractive ornamental plant. As they planted more and more of them, little by little, atala hairstreaks started to appear on them. Now a law protects the limited population. Though this was an accident, it shows how planting the right vegetation can sometimes save an insect. Cutting down grasslands to grow crops has endangered once common grass-dwelling butterflies, such as the regal fritillary and the zebra swallowtail. Marshlands that have been drained for farming have endangered the large copper butterfly. These brilliant-orange creatures became extinct in England but were successfully reintroduced by replanting the vegetation on which they depended.

The black-and-yellow Corsican swallowtail, a family of 200 butterfly species living only on the Mediterranean islands of Corsica and Sardinia, are in decline. They live in forests of an elevation higher than 200 feet, feeding and laying eggs on the leaves of various woodland plants. They are collected and sold to tourists at such a rate that this alone would endanger them. But added to their problems, one of their main foods is a plant that farmers are trying to destroy because they believe it is poisonous to livestock.

The Jamaican giant swallowtail—with an impressive six-inch wingspan—is the largest butterfly in the Americas. Because they prefer wet limestone forests, their habitat is also being invaded by people. They used to live on half of Jamaica, but land clearing for agriculture has destroyed much of their grounds. Even in more remote places on the island, bauxite mining has destroyed their habitat. These remarkable insects now hide in two fairly out-of-the-way areas, but they are still hunted down as a favorite and very commercial specimen for collectors.

Because it is so beautiful and considered a gem for a collector, the tiny Karner blue butterfly (with a one-inch wing span) is increasingly rare. Nabokov was celebrated for his studies of Karner blues. Their pale-lavender color and the splashes of orange on the female wings make fine specimens and, naturally, collectors wanted those. But a bigger problem is the destruction of their essential habitat, wild lupine.

The Lotis blue butterfly of California is considered the rarest butterfly in North America. Although on the endangered species list, little is known about it because there have been very few opportunities to observe it. It is unknown why they have become so scarce, but they were never commonly seen butterflies. The species might even be extinct, since there has been no reported sighting since 1983. But it is believed that a few still exist in remote places.

The centuries-old passion for professional collections has expanded. The British Museum collection now has more than 30 million insects, including 8.5 million butterflies and moths. Sadly, such large old collections preserve a record of species that have vanished. But beyond such museum collections there are many amateur hobbyists all over the world collecting butterflies, and this is becoming a problem. Rare butterflies are killed and sold to collectors. Human development drives butterflies from the more accessible areas. But they are also hunted in more remote mountains for collectors. In India and Thailand, a large mountain butterfly, the Bhutan glory, is becoming rare because of collectors.

Some governments and various private organizations have been trying to save butterflies. The International Union for Conservation of Nature (IUCN) issues the Red List, which notes species in trouble. One group that tries to protect butterflies in the United States is called the Xerces Society, named after a California butterfly that became extinct in 1941.

Reserves have been established around the world to nurture struggling species. These butterflies can sometimes be reintroduced to places where they became extinct, which is how Britain got back its coppers. Reserves also farm some popular collectors' species so that collectors won't hunt them in the wild. But the problem remains that if the habitat is destroyed, there is no place in the wild for the butterflies to live.

In addition to farms, there are butterfly ranches, commercial operations that breed butterflies near wild areas and sell them around the world. Ranchers entice wild butterflies to lay eggs on their ranches, and because they protect them, they have a fairly high survival rate—far higher than in nature.

Butterfly ranching is a big business in Papua New Guinea, an independent Pacific country near Australia. The government regulates the business and assures the preservation of the species as well as keeping the prices high. There are also ranches in East Africa and Central America. Zoos, scientists, and collectors create a large market for butterflies.

Butterfly breeding is also catching on in the United States. For less than $100, you can buy a dozen monarch butterflies, packaged to be released at just the right moment at a wedding or another festivity. To biologists, transporting a species to another habitat where it can mix with a different group is a huge mistake. They believe it can weaken or even destroy the species. Several species of butterfly are used in these kinds of events, but monarchs appear to be most popular. They are one of nine species that US law allows to be transported commercially across state lines. Thousands of monarchs are features in American weddings every year.

CONCLUSION

21

STOPS ALONG THE ROAD TO LONELINESS

ONE OF DARWIN'S IMPORTANT principles, as he simply put it, is "Rarity . . . is the precursor to extinction." If there are not many individuals left in a species, the species will become extinct. We might be concerned, but Darwin did not see extinction as a problem. He thought it was what was supposed to happen. New species are created and old ones die out. It was his belief that the Earth always maintained the same number of species.

That's not what is happening anymore. Between the species that have gone extinct and the ones that have become so rare that they probably will, we are losing species at a faster rate than we are gaining them. And this decline in variety, what scientists call a decline in biodiversity, threatens most of the survivors.

There are many insects besides butterflies, beetles, and bees that are disappearing. Vanishing wetlands in the northern Midwest have put the Hine's emerald dragonfly, named for its bright green eyes, on the endangered species list.

Many doubt that the Hawaiian pomace fly will survive. This fruit fly's larvae thrive only in native vegetation, which is being overtaken by foreign arrivals and livestock. Plant species are also going extinct.

In 1987, the United Nations released an important report titled "Our Common Future," a document that defined the phrase "sustainable development." This is economic development carried out in a nondestructive manner so it can continue to be pursued without diminishing the natural order. The report declared that our current economic development could not be maintained, because of the damage it has been causing. It also singled out plants and insects as showing particularly alarming rates of extinction. The text reads, "There is a growing consensus that species are disappearing at rates never before witnessed on the planet."

Since at least 72 percent of known animal species in the world are insects, their role in the natural order is enormous. Their absence would be devastating. E. O. Wilson wrote, "So important are insects and other land-dwelling arthropods, that if all were to disappear, humanity probably could not last more than a few months." This is a more measured voice of doom than Albert Einstein's prediction: "If the bee disappeared off the surface of the globe then man would only have four years of life left."

What scientists cannot tell us with much accuracy is how many species have been lost or even how many are at risk of being lost. That is not surprising, since they also can't tell us how many species even exist. According to the IUCN, 72 insects in the world are already extinct. Assuming this is accurate, many other dependent species are endangered by this loss. An American program, the Natural Heritage Program, which provides the public with information about the state of species, thinks the news is worse. They say possibly 160 insects may already be extinct in just the United States.

Many scientists do not trust these numbers. They believe that the truth is even worse. Perhaps thousands of insects have become extinct in North America and Europe alone in the past two centuries, a period of great human population increase and habitat destruction. But in the tropics, far less known, and with far richer insect life, the destruction has certainly been much greater. Scientists have examined insect collections dating back only to the 1970s, and discovered insects for which they cannot find a living sample today.

Some common and widespread insects of the nineteenth century seem to no longer exist, such as the Rocky Mountain grasshopper, also known as the locust. In the nineteenth century, the American West had huge numbers of them, as did southern Canada. In 1875 a swarm of them covered an area 1,800 miles long and 110 miles wide, an area as big as two large western states. The swarm was estimated to be made up of more than 10 billion insects. It takes a lot of food to sustain swarms like that one, comparable to what a large herd of bison would eat. They cleaned out entire fields of crops at once. Farmers described the sound of a billion little jaws chomping up their grain. Even if farmers had covered their crops with cloth, the locusts would have gobbled that down too.

They were a curse. Farmers lit fires and did everything else they could think of to drive them away. Nothing worked.

But they seem to be gone now. No locust has been sighted since 1902, in Canada. This is the largest and most rapid die-off of insects in recorded history, and no one is certain why it happened. The effort to be rid of them was intense but unsuccessful, so what did destroy them? Again, the prime suspect is habitat loss. Farmers and ranchers changed the land. They flattened it, clearing grassland and forests. The loss of locusts is not mourned. But scientists wonder: If such a large, important population could die off so quickly from changes in the land, how many tiny populations that are not even being watched are also vanishing?

Habitat destruction is one of the major causes for our disappearing insects. It can be more easily observed and is better documented in newer areas of development, like the southeastern United States and California. We don't know what damage we did in other places a century or more earlier. It is well-known that San Francisco, by entirely covering a coastal dune ecosystem, drove three dune butterfly species to extinction. All that remains of that ecosystem are other butterflies, hanging on near to extinction, on the San Bruno Mountain.

How many insects, birds, plants, and mammals were driven to extinction when the fertile wetlands of the Hudson River estuary became completely paved over and turned into New York City? There was once a wildcat population in Manhattan, and Coney Island was named for its population of wild coney (rabbits), which are now gone.

Human activity has always been destructive—from the first campfires to hunters to fields plowed. But in the past, our human population was so small, none of this damage seemed noticeable. In evolution, humans have been conditioned to pursue these activities. Experience has taught us that these actions advance the species. We are conditioned to do these developmental activities for the good of our own species, in the same way forager bees gather nectar and pollen for the good of the hive. The problem is that despite frequent damaging wars and periodic destructive epidemics, the human population is forever increasing. While today's demands for development are greater than ever before, so are the risks.

Stoneflies are a common insect living in fast-moving rivers or on their banks. Most fly fishermen are familiar with them, because trout like to eat them and will often chase an artificial fly that resembles one. And yet stoneflies are another example of a common insect that is disappearing. If we lose our aquatic insects, there will be no more trout, char, and salmon.

Damming the Columbia River system between Oregon, Washington, and Idaho has created the electric power needed to develop cities and the land to grow more food for an increasing population. But changing that water system has destroyed stoneflies and tiger beetles. Damming has damaged the great salmon of the area as well.

Many insects, such as stoneflies, which live partly on the banks, are also destroyed by construction on the water. People think it is a lovely thing to build a home on the river, but they may be killing the river.

The ecological and emotional impact of endangering the magnificent king and sockeye salmon is upsetting people far more than the loss of stoneflies and tiger beetles. That is just the way we are. We have to start thinking not just in terms of saving our favorite animals but saving the ecosystem as a whole. Without a healthy system, nothing can be saved.

And this takes us to our truly favorite species, human beings. Without any insects, we probably could not survive. But let us imagine life with just fewer insects, a lot fewer, so that little pollination is happening. That would mean very little food was being produced. Honeybees alone are responsible for the production of 90 common foods. Fruits, certain garden plants such as tomatoes, and some grains would be very limited and expensive to produce. Some grains such as wheat use the wind rather than insects to disperse their pollen. Barley is wind-pollinated. Walnuts are also wind-pollinated, but almonds would probably be a rarity. A single piece of fruit, a peach or an apple, would be so expensive that only the rich could afford to occasionally eat one.

Without enough insects to pollinate a large crop, cotton, one of the most common and affordable fabrics, would also become rare and expensive. Little meat or dairy would be produced, and milk, cheese, and yogurt would also be luxuries. Ice cream would become a very rare treat, and even if you had the money and could find some, it would not be chocolate, vanilla, or most fruit flavors unless they were artificial. Without the tiny chocolate midge there would be no cocoa plants. Perhaps dairy farmers will give up on grain and turn to completely grass feeding. It would be a cheaper way to raise cows, but prices would have to come up because production would be much smaller—and it would probably lead to further habitat destruction.

There would probably be a shortage of grass, because many grasses depend on insects. Insects condition the soil for roots to grow. In fact, without insects, few plants would do well, because it is the insects that dig and tunnel and maintain the quality and texture of soil so that it is suitable for roots to grow. All the beautiful plants are trying to attract pollinators. Wind-pollinated plants needn't bother—so most of the survivors would be less attractive. There would be no flowers. Also, wind-pollinated plants are the ones that carry allergens. Many plants would simply die out, as would many birds and some mammals, reptiles, and amphibians. It is not known what could live in this diminished world.

A world with fewer insects would be a world with even stronger divisions between rich and poor than there are today. A small group of the very wealthy would eat quite well, and a huge mass of people would be starving. History has taught us that this is a recipe for violent upheavals and great political unrest. When there is a lack of food, societies collapse.

And this is the optimistic scenario. Remember Darwin: the fewer species, the harder it is for any of them to survive. The less biodiversity there is, the less biodiversity there will be, and the spiral keeps descending. The extinction of a large number of insects, and subsequently a large number of plants, could lead to the extinction of many bird, amphibian, and mammal species that live from those insects or plants. Already, large numbers of species of insect-eating birds and frogs have died off. And that would undo the animals that depend on those birds, amphibians, and mammals. At the same time, there would be a huge unseen die-off of fungi, protozoa, and bacteria. Those losses would also have serious consequences for larger life. Without fungi, there would be no more antibiotics.

If insects disappear, there is no way to know whether or not humans would survive. Willing to eat anything, cockroaches might have a better chance. Humans are also fairly omnivorous, and with the largest brain in the animal kingdom by far, we are extremely resourceful. We might be able to figure out how to live in a world with no flowers and few animals. We might even find more efficient ways to pollinate, though the fruits of these plants would be more precious than diamonds.

Scientists have divided the Earth's development into 20 different periods of time. For example, about 4 billion years ago there was the Hadean period. This was before there were rocks on Earth and when the entire solar system was just forming. Later, about 542 to 488.3 million years ago, came the very eventful Cambrian Period. Sometimes called the Cambrian explosion, it was at this time that a huge variety of living creatures emerged to create a diverse system of life. The Jurassic period is familiar to many, well-known for its dinosaurs. Many flowers and insects first appeared during the Cretaceous period. The Holocene period runs from 11,700 years ago to the present. In this latest period, which began after the Ice Age ended, human beings started to play an important role in the natural environment. This period in which we now live is sometimes called the Age of Man.

But scientists are beginning to talk of a new age, the Anthropocene Age, which means "the New Human Age." These scientists are describing the time period in which humans have started to overtake and destroy a large number of other animals. Scientists argue among themselves about when this new age began. Some say it started in the twentieth century, but others think it began earlier, in the nineteenth century with the Industrial Revolution. And then there are scientists who believe the New Human

Age actually began thousands of years ago, with the beginning of agriculture. Without a doubt, the world was forever changed when humans started to manipulate nature by farming.

In any event, this new age is well underway. These are the times in which we live: we are now killing off animals, insects included, at an alarming rate. As a warning, E. O. Wilson termed this new age "The Age of Loneliness."

From the biological point of view, it is imaginable that one species could so overproduce and overconsume and use up so much habitat in ways incompatible with other species, that there would be nothing left for all the other species. It has always been the existence of natural enemies that has kept populations in check. But suppose one species was so successful in defeating its enemies, carnivores and bacteria, that nothing checked its expansion. Darwin wrote, "There is no exception to the rule that every organic being naturally increases at so high a rate that, if not destroyed, the Earth would soon be covered by the progeny of a single pair." In other words, one species—or even a single line from one species—could take over the world and threaten the survival of the rest of the natural order. That is why nature creates enemies for most every species.

We seem to be that species taking over the world from all the other species. Even if we could, with our extraordinary resourcefulness, learn to survive in such a diminished world, it would certainly be, as Wilson said, "an age of loneliness." Wouldn't it be better to use that resourcefulness to learn how to survive with all we have?

Otherwise, we have evolved to be intelligent but not intelligent enough. We know that evolution makes mistakes and species die out and others take over. Was intelligence a mistake, a feature that doesn't work out and ensure survival? After we are gone, will species that evolved without any intelligence, such as bacteria, fungi, protists, and archaea, live on more successfully?

22
KiLLER BiOLOGY

IN THE ASSORTMENT OF ways that nature can be destroyed, one of the most solvable is the problem of pesticides. Pests, insects that destroy crops, are a real problem that has to be dealt with for farms to earn enough to survive. Further, agriculture must be productive enough to provide the food we need for our growing world population. Since an estimated 12 percent of the world's crops are destroyed each year by insects and mites, farmers need a pest-control strategy.

Pesticides need to be target-specific, not general poisons that kill everything in the area. It would also help pollinators if farmers did not spray pesticides while crops were in bloom. Farmers could also plant habitat, taking up very little space. Making hedgerows around fields is a tradition in some countries, and it creates homes for helpful insects.

But it is not certain that poisonous pesticides are needed at all. There is still the time-tested strategy of biological control. This idea is far older that pesticides. For example, many farmers, rather than laying poison around their homes to get rid of mice and thereby endangering their children and livestock, simply get a cat or two because cats efficiently kill mice. Almost all pests have natural enemies—like ladybugs that eat aphids.

Of course, there are risks to bringing in enemies. After all, that is what the *I* stands for in HIPPO: invasive species. The most famous case of such an ecological misstep was when mongooses from India were brought to the Caribbean to rid the cane fields of rats. The sharp-toothed, long-tailed mammals did a great job, and in little time the rats were gone. Then they started in on many other native species, such as ground-nesting birds, lizards, and sea turtles. Now the mongooses are the pests, and no one seems sure what to do about them.

In general, scientists work on biological control very carefully, and there are few cases of it leading to problematic invasions. Usually the pests are foreign species that have arrived by accident, like the cottony cushion scale in the California citrus groves.

Many of the pests that plague American crops are not native insects. This is largely true in other countries as well. It is rare for an insect living in its native environment to be out of control. Nature provides enemies to keep them in check. But insects move in that weren't meant to be part of the local ecosystem, and they may have an unexpected hunger for a certain crop and a lack of natural enemies. Back in their former home, there were other insects or animals, or viruses that attacked them and kept their population from becoming dangerously large. But in their new home, there are no enemies to control their numbers. There are two possible solutions: kill them with chemical poisons or bring in their natural enemy. The natural enemy often comes from the same place as the pest.

Bringing in natural enemies was the only option available until DDT ushered in the age of pesticides in the 1940s. Once pesticides arrived, their advantages were immediately recognized. The first was psychological. When a farmer purchased and sprayed a chemical, they looked for a quick, sure, and immediate result. Introducing a beetle or other insect would mean waiting for results. And it is well-known that certain pesticide-spraying campaigns have had excellent results, including progress against mosquito-borne illnesses such as malaria.

There is a notable negative side to pesticides. Aside from the fact that they tend to ravage the natural order, killing many living organisms that we would like to keep, we are also one of their victims. Every year, as many as two hundred thousand people are poisoned by pesticides.

It is difficult to evaluate all the consequences of pesticides since, after use, many keep their toxicity for years, penetrating water systems. Also, target pests build immunity to some pesticides. So while at first the results seem spectacular, over time the pesticide becomes less effective unless the dosage is increased.

But an aphid will never develop immunity to a ladybug. Placing a natural enemy in the field will usually not completely destroy the pest. That is not how nature works, and it is one of the psychological reasons that pesticides are more satisfying to humans: they completely wipe out their target, whereas natural enemies only control the population.

There are several hundred viruses that attack insects and mites, and there are a number of useful bacteria. Fungi were among the first organisms used for biological control.

Officially, the technique called "biological control" began in 1888 with the successful campaign against the cottony cushion scale in the California citrus groves. After their valuable crops were saved from this highly destructive pest, farmers started seeking more such solutions.

There had been many attempts before this in history. The ancient Chinese kept ants in their citrus groves to take on boring beetles and hungry caterpillars. The practice dated back to 324 BCE. Carl Linnaeus once said in a lecture:

> Since people noted the damage done by insects, thought
> has been given to ways of getting rid of them, but so far
> nobody has thought of getting rid of insects with insects.
> Every insect has its predator, which follows and
> destroys it.

Not to contradict the great biologist, but actually a great many had given thought to it. It just didn't strike farmers as a serious idea until a major commercial crop was saved by it. Then almost everyone wanted an insect predator to save their crops.

There are huge families of parasites with different genera preying on different insects. Many beetles are effective insect predators, though a few are classified as pests because they eat crops. Ants are also used for control, though sometimes they too are considered pests to be controlled.

The Ichneumonidae family, or parasites, are lethal to various insects.

This family has more species than there are vertebrates—that is all mammals, reptiles, amphibians, fish, and birds combined. There are also non-insects like the giant toad, which has been effective against certain species of scarab beetles that devastate crops. Certain fish and a few lizards have been effective against mosquitoes. The mosquitofish has been installed all over the world because it devours mosquito larvae. Myna birds help control locusts.

Bedbugs are an interesting dilemma. True bugs, they bite people and leave red welts. People have always hated them. In recent years, large infestations have broken out in cities, including New York. Landlords, tenants, property owners, and hotel owners can get rid of them by hiring experts who come in and thoroughly spray their homes with poison. Some people, especially with small children, worry about giving this heavy dose of poison to their homes.

In Europe, as early as 1776, bedbug infestations were controlled by introducing the pentatomid bug or *Picromerus bidens*. Also a true bug— order Hemiptera—it eats aphids, beetles, the sap of plants, but also bedbugs. Release a group of these tiny green-and-gray bugs in your apartment, and you will soon have no more bedbugs. Though these other bugs won't bite you, people would rather poison their home than live with these new critters. People just don't like bugs.

23
WHAT CAN I DO?

THERE ARE TIMES WHEN a community pulls together to save an insect. It happened in a village in New York's Adirondack Mountains, Wilton. It is an area known for its rural beauty, but in the 1970s, life was changing. A wide interstate highway was built. Then more and more houses and shopping malls were built.

Some wanted the new development and others didn't—but they could all agree on one thing: they were sad that their beautiful blue butterfly, the Karner blue, was disappearing. The reason was that the wild blue lupine, those vertical blue-and-purple stalks of flowers, were vanishing. In the 1990s, citizens in the community started donating fields and woodlands to the Wilton Wildlife Preserve. The local people, businesses, and schools got involved. The Nature Conservancy, a Virginia-based environmental organization with roots going back 100 years, helped out. Schools gave children wild lupine seeds to plant. People started their own home butterfly gardens. Now the Karner blue is back, and other species are also profiting from its presence.

There has been a lot of talk about reducing footprints, especially a carbon footprint, which means the amount of carbon your activities cause, which contributes to climate change. But there is a broader discussion to be had: your impact on nature. The first thing to understand is that, without a doubt, you will make a footprint. You are a species in the natural order, living in an ecosystem, unavoidably connected to nature, and so of course everything you do has an impact. The point is to make your footprint as positive as possible.

There are things you can do to help insects—which in the long run helps all of us.

- For one, speaking of footprints, stop the popular and disturbing habit of stamping on insects to pointlessly kill them when you see them.
- Plant gardens with flowers that attract pollinators. Build nests for certain bees and butterflies. A bee garden can be built in a backyard or in flower boxes on the roof of a city building.
- In areas with firefly populations, use low lighting at night. Avoid light pollution, which means no floodlights. This is a good rule whether you are trying to attract fireflies or not.

- Leave "natural litter" around trees. This is twigs, leaves, the kind of stuff found on forest floors. This is where fireflies like to deposit eggs. Provide fireflies with standing water, such as a manmade pond. Swimming pools do not help, since they are treated with chemicals.

- Ask your family not to use pesticides on their lawns or gardens, and to only use natural fertilizers. Grow long grasses and leave part of your lawn unmowed. If you want fireflies, you have to appreciate a different look. Fireflies live in tall grass.

- Though butterfly science no longer depends on the amateur collector, it still depends on amateurs. The effort to save the monarch is managed by a few scientists rallying hundreds of volunteers. Thousands of volunteers have been used to monitor and count monarch locations and migration. Check out:
  ○ North American Butterfly Association (naba.org)
  ○ Monarch Watch (monarchwatch.org)
  ○ Southwest Monarch Study (swmonarchs.org)

- For information on building a butterfly garden or on conservation of butterflies, bees, or other pollinators, contact the Xerces Society at xerces.org.

- Cornell University's Department of Entomology is looking for ladybug-spotting volunteers, inviting kids to become bug spotters for their Lost Ladybug Project. They ask you to go out looking for ladybugs, then take a digital picture and send it to ladybug@cornell.edu with information on where it was caught, when, and what type of habitat. This is a great way to become part of a large, ongoing scientific study. For more information, visit lostladybug.org.

Bees like a wide variety of flowers: tomatoes, sunflowers, asters, clover, marigolds, roses, hyacinth, snapdragons, delphinium, sage, mint, oregano, buttercups, goldenrod, and many more. If possible, you should provide some bare dirt for nesting, and logs or branches with some holes drilled in them.

Experience has shown that bees flourish on city roofs. (City dwellers have to look into this, because some places have ordinances against bee raising.) Bees do well on New York rooftops, and quite a few bees are Manhattanites.

The huge glass Javits Center in Manhattan has a 6.75-acre rooftop with plants and flowers welcoming over 17 bird species, 5 bat species, and 300,000 honeybees.

If you do learn to raise bees, you could feed them lemongrass or spearmint oil. Bees love both, and these oil treats act like bee vitamins, making them stronger and more resistant to mites and viruses. This is a good alternative to using pesticides in a hive; the bee mites increasingly build up immunity to pesticides.

Make sure there are no pesticides in the soil or the seeds. Some seeds are "painted" with pesticides.

There are many websites for advice on how to plant honeybee-friendly gardens such as the Honeybee Conservancy, Plan Bee Central, and many others.

We need to participate. We have to save insects to save the planet. But there is a second issue, almost as important—saving the beauty of the planet. This means not only saving the chirps and buzz of a summer's day. We learn that the natural beauty of a flower or an insect is for a purpose, not just for our pleasure. But there is also a deep pleasure in it. If we take the time to look, there is dazzling beauty in the flight of a bee, the pattern of a butterfly wing, even the colors of some beetles, and the flash of a firefly. And they all have great stories that can thrill or inspire.

BIBLIOGRAPHY

BOOKS FOR YOUNG READERS

Coughlan, Cheryl. *Fireflies*. Mankato, MN: Capstone Press, 1999.

Coughlan, Cheryl. *Ladybugs*. Mankato, MN: Capstone Press, 1999.

Green, Jen. *Butterflies (Endangered!)*. New York: Cavendish Square Publishing, 1999.

Johnson, Sylvia A. *Ladybugs*. Minneapolis: Lerner Publishing Group, 1984.

Kohn, Bernice. *Fireflies*. Englewood Cliffs, NJ: Prentice Hall, 1968.

Pringle, Laurence. *An Extraordinary Life: The Story of a Monarch Butterfly*. New York: Orchard Books, 1996.

GENERAL READING

It takes many books to write a book. These are all books that were used to research this book and are suggested for the curious who want to know more. The degree of difficulty varies. Von Frisch can be difficult. Darwin is much more readable. Stephen Jay Gould, Oliver Sacks, and E. O. Wilson are scientists who are very readable. So are many of these other authors.

Benjamin, Alison, and Brian McCallum. *A World Without Bees*. London: Guardian Books, 2008.

Boyd, Brian, and Robert Michael Pyle, eds. *Nabokov's Butterflies: Unpublished and Uncollected Writings*. Boston: Beacon Press, 2000.

Buchmann, Stephen. *The Reason for Flowers: Their History, Culture, Biology, and How They Change Our Lives*. New York: Scribner, 2015.

Buchmann, Stephen L., and Gary Paul Nabhan. *The Forgotten Pollinators*. Washington, D.C.: Island Press, 1996.

Burkhardt, Frederick, ed. *Origins: Selected Letters of Charles Darwin, 1822–1859*. Cambridge: Cambridge University Press, 2008.

Carson, Rachel. *Silent Spring*. Boston: Houghton Mifflin, 1962.

Darwin, Charles. *On the Various Contrivances by Which British and Foreign Orchids Are Fertilised by Insects; and on the Good Effects of Intercrossing*. London: John Murray, 1862.

Darwin, Charles. *The Various Contrivances by Which Orchids Are Fertilised by Insects* [1885 edition]. Honolulu: University Press of the Pacific, 2003.

Debauch, Paul, and David Rosen. *Biological Control by Natural Enemies*. Cambridge: Cambridge University Press, 1991.

Droege, Sam, and Laurence Packer. *Bees: An Up-Close Look at Pollinators Around the World*. Minneapolis: Voyageur Press, 2015.

Gould, James L., and Carol Grant Gould. *The Honey Bee*. New York: Scientific American Library, 1988.

Gould, Stephen Jay. *Bully for Brontosaurus: Reflections in Natural History*. New York: W. W. Norton, 1991.

Gould, Stephen Jay. *Eight Little Piggies: Reflections in Natural History*. New York: Trafalgar Square, 1993.

Gould, Stephen Jay. *The Flamingo's Smile: Reflections in Natural History*. New York: W. W. Norton, 1985.

Gould, Stephen Jay. *Wonderful Life: The Burgess Shale and the Nature of History*. New York: W. W. Norton, 1989.

Heinrich, Bernd. *Bumblebee Economics*. Cambridge, MA: Harvard University Press, 2004.

Holt, Vincent M. *Why Not Eat Insects?* Whitstable, UK: Pryor Publications, 1992 (original 1885).

Lewis, Sara. *Silent Sparks: The Wondrous World of Fireflies*. Princeton, NJ: Princeton University Press, 2016.

Lewis, Trevor, ed. *Insect Communication: 12th Symposium of the Royal Entomological Society of London*. London: Academic Press, 1984.

Lindauer, Martin. *Communication Among Social Bees*. Cambridge, MA: Harvard University Press, 1961.

Manos-Jones, Maraleen. *The Spirit of Butterflies: Myth, Magic, and Art*. New York: Harry N. Abrams, 2000.

Oberhauser, Karen S., Kelly R. Nail, and Sonia Altizer, eds. *Monarchs in a Changing World: Biology and Conservation of an Iconic Butterfly*. Ithaca, NY: Cornell University Press, 2015.

Oberhauser, Karen S., and Michelle J. Solensky, eds. *The Monarch Butterfly: Biology and Conservation*. Ithaca, NY: Cornell University Press, 2004.

Prum, Richard O. *The Evolution of Beauty: How Darwin's Forgotten Theory of Mate Choice Shapes the Animal World—and Us*. New York: Doubleday, 2017.

Pyle, Robert Michael. *Chasing Monarchs: Migrating with the Butterflies of Passage*. New York: Houghton Mifflin Harcourt, 1999.

Raffles, Hugh. *Insectopedia*. New York: Pantheon, 2010.

Resh, Vincent H., and Ring T. Cardé, eds. *Encyclopedia of Insects*. Boston: Academic Press, 2003.

Rothschild, Miriam. *Butterfly Cooing Like a Dove*. New York: Doubleday, 1991.

Russell, Sharman Apt. *An Obsession with Butterflies: Our Long Love Affair with a Singular Insect.* New York: Perseus, 2003.

Sacks, Oliver. *The River of Consciousness.* New York: Alfred A. Knopf, 2017.

Salmon, Michael A. *The Aurelian Legacy: British Butterflies and Their Collectors.* Berkeley: University of California Press, 2001.

Schacker, Michael. *A Spring without Bees: How Colony Collapse Disorder Has Endangered Our Food Supply.* Guilford, CT: Lyons Press, 2008.

Schappert, Phil. *The Last Monarch Butterfly: Conserving the Monarch Butterfly in a Brave New World.* Buffalo, NY: Firefly Books, 2004.

Schappert, Phil. *A World for Butterflies: Their Lives, Behavior and Future.* Buffalo, NY: Firefly Books, 2005.

Simmonds, Peter Lund. *The Curiosities of Food: Or the Dainties and Delicacies of Different Nations Obtained from the Animal Kingdom.* Berkeley: Ten Speed Press, 2001.

Skutch, Alexander F. *Origins of Nature's Beauty.* Austin: University of Texas Press, 1992.

Urquhart, F. A. *The Monarch Butterfly.* Toronto: University of Toronto Press, 1960.

Von Frisch, Karl. Leigh E. Chadwick, trans. *The Dance Language and Orientation of Bees.* Cambridge, Harvard University Press, 1967.

Von Frisch, Karl. Dora Ilse, trans. *The Dancing Bees.* London: Methuen, 1954.

Wilson, E. O., ed. *Biodiversity.* Washington, D.C.: National Academy of Sciences, 1988.

Wilson, E. O., Marjorie L. Reaka-Kudla, and Don E. Wilson, eds. *Biodiversity II: Understanding and Protecting Our Biological Resources.* Washington, D.C.: Joseph Henry Press, 1996.

Wilson, E. O. *The Creation: An Appeal to Save Life on Earth*. New York: W. W. Norton, 2006.

Wilson, E. O., ed. *From So Simple a Beginning: Darwin's Four Great Books*. New York: W. W. Norton, 2005.

Wilson, E. O. *The Meaning of Human Existence*. New York: Liveright Publishing, 2014.

The most useful website for biology is the Encyclopedia of Life, eol.org, put together by leading biologists as a constantly updateable encyclopedia of biological knowledge.

INDEX